More than **200,000** student reviews on nearly **7,000** schools!

SEE IT ALL ON COLLEGEPROWLER.COM!

This book only offers a glimpse at our extensive coverage of one school out of thousands across the country. Visit *collegeprowler.com* to view our full library of content for FREE! Our site boasts thousands of photos and videos, interactive search tools, more reviews, and expanded content on nearly 7,000 schools.

CONNECT WITH SCHOOLS
Connect with the schools you are most interested in and discover new schools that match your interests.

FIND SCHOLARSHIPS
We give away $2,000 each month and offer personalized matches from a database of more than 3.2 million other scholarships!

SELECT A MAJOR
We have information on every major in the country to help you choose your degree and plan your career.

USE OUR TOOLS TO HELP YOU CHOOSE
Compare schools side-by-side, estimate your chances of admission, and get personalized school recommendations.

To get started, visit <u>collegeprowler.com/register</u>

The Big Book of Colleges

Choosing the perfect school can be an overwhelming challenge. Luckily, our *Big Book of Colleges* makes that task a little less daunting. We've packed it with overviews of our full library of single-school guides—more than 400 of the nation's top schools—giving you some much-needed perspective on your search.

BIG BOOK OF COLLEGES '12
Paperback 7.75" X 10", 900+ pages
$29.95 Retail
ISBN: 978-1-4274-0326-1

*To order your copy,
visit collegeprowler.com/store*

Valparaiso University

Valparaiso, IN

Written by Amber Will, Matthew A. Stevens

Edited by the College Prowler Team

ISBN # 978-1-4274-0682-8

©Copyright 2011 College Prowler

All Rights Reserved
Printed in the U.S.A.
www.collegeprowler.com

Last updated: 3/24/2011

College Prowler®
5001 Baum Blvd.
Suite 750
Pittsburgh, PA 15213

Phone: (800) 290-2682
Fax: (800) 772-4972
E-Mail: info@collegeprowler.com
Web: www.collegeprowler.com

©Copyright 2011 College Prowler.

All rights reserved. No part of this work may be reproduced or transmitted in any form or by any means, including but not limited to, photocopy, recording, or any information storage and retrieval systems, without the express written permission of College Prowler®.

College Prowler® is not sponsored by, affiliated with, or approved by Valparaiso University in any way.

College Prowler® strives faithfully to record its sources. As the reader understands, opinions, impressions, and experiences are necessarily personal and unique. Accordingly, there are, and can be, no guarantees of future satisfaction extended to the reader.

How this all started...

When I was trying to find the perfect college, I used every resource that was available to me. I went online to visit school Web sites; I talked with my high school guidance counselor; I read book after book; I hired a private counselor. Sure, this was all very helpful, but nothing really told me what life was like at the schools I cared about. These sources weren't giving me enough information to be totally confident in my decision.

In all my research, there were only two ways to get the information I wanted.

The first was to physically visit the campuses and see if things were really how the brochures described them, but this was quite expensive and not always feasible. The second involved a missing ingredient: the students. Actually talking to a few students at those schools gave me a taste of the information that I needed so badly. The problem was that I wanted more but didn't have access to enough people.

In the end, I weighed my options and decided on a school that felt right and had a great academic reputation, but truth be told, the choice was still very much a crapshoot. I had done as much research as any other student, but was I 100 percent positive that I had picked the school of my dreams?

Absolutely not.

My dream in creating College Prowler was to build a resource that people can use with confidence. My own college search experience taught me the importance of gaining true insider insight; that's why the majority of this guide is composed of quotes from actual students. After all, shouldn't you hear about a school from the people who know it best?

I hope you enjoy reading this book as much as we've enjoyed putting it together. Tell me what you think when you get a chance. I'd love to hear your college selection stories.

Luke Skurman
CEO and Co-Founder
luke@collegeprowler.com

Welcome to College Prowler®

When we created College Prowler, we felt it was critical that our content was unbiased and unaffiliated with any college or university. We think it's important that our readers get honest information and a realistic impression of the student opinions on any campus—that's why if any aspect of a particular school is terrible, we (unlike a campus brochure) intend to publish it. While we do keep an eye out for the occasional extremist—the cheerleader or the cynic—we take pride in letting the students tell it like it is. We strive to create a book that's as representative as possible of each particular campus. Our books cover both the good and the bad, and whether the survey responses point to recurring trends or a variation in opinion, these sentiments are directly and proportionally expressed through our guides.

College Prowler guidebooks are in the hands of students throughout the entire process of their creation. Because you can't make student-written guides without the students, we have students at each campus who help write, randomly survey their peers, edit, layout, and perform accuracy checks on every book that we publish. From the very beginning, student writers gather the most up-to-date stats, facts, and inside information on their colleges. They fill each section with student quotes and summarize the findings in editorial reviews. In addition, each school receives a collection of letter grades (A through F) that reflect student opinion and help to represent contentment or satisfaction for each of our 20 specific categories. Just as in grade school, the higher the mark the more content or more satisfied the students are with the particular category.

Each book is the result of endless student contributions, hundreds of pages of research and writing, and countless hours of hard work. All of this has led to the creation of a student information network that stretches across the nation to every school that we cover. It's no easy accomplishment, but it's the reason that our guides are such a great resource.

When reading our books and looking at our grades, keep in mind that every college is different and that the students who make up each school are not uniform—as a result, it is important to assess schools on a case-by-case basis. Because it's impossible to summarize an entire school with a single number or description, each book provides a dialogue, not a decision, that's made up of 20 different topics and hundreds of student quotes. In the end, we hope that this guide will serve as a valuable tool in your college selection process. Enjoy!

The College Prowler Team

VALPARAISO UNIVERSITY
Table of Contents

By the Numbers.................... **1**

Academics **4**

Local Atmosphere **12**

Health & Safety.................. **18**

Computers.......................... **24**

Facilities.............................. **30**

Campus Dining.................. **36**

Off-Campus Dining **43**

Campus Housing **54**

Off-Campus Housing......... **63**

Diversity.............................. **68**

Guys & Girls....................... **74**

Athletics.............................. **80**

Nightlife.............................. **88**

Greek Life **94**

Drug Scene...................... **100**

Campus Strictness **105**

Parking............................. **110**

Transportation **116**

Weather **121**

Report Card Summary ... **125**

Overall Experience **126**

The Inside Scoop............ **131**

Jobs & Internships.......... **137**

Alumni & Post-Grads **140**

Student Organizations.... **142**

The Best **144**

The Worst **145**

Visiting............................. **146**

Words to Know............... **148**

By the Numbers

School Contact
Valparaiso University
US Highway 30 and Sturdy Road
1700 Chapel Dr.
Valparaiso, IN 46383

Control:
Private Non-Profit

Academic Calendar:
Semester

Religious Affiliation:
Protestant

Founded:
1859

Web Site:
www.valpo.edu

Main Phone:
(219) 464-5000

Student Body
Full-Time Undergraduates:
2,733

Part-Time Undergraduates:
155

Total Male Undergraduates:
1,463

Total Female Undergraduates:
1,627

Admissions
Acceptance Rate:
91%

Total Applicants:
2,932

Total Acceptances:
2,674

Freshman Enrollment:
671

Yield (% of admitted students who enroll):
25%

Transfer Applications Received:
245

Transfer Applications Accepted:
220

Transfer Students Enrolled:
119

Transfer Application Acceptance Rate:
90%

SAT I or ACT Required?
Either

SAT I Range (25th–75th Percentile):
1460–1860

SAT I Verbal Range (25th–75th Percentile):
480–630

SAT I Math Range (25th–75th Percentile):
500–620

SAT I Writing Range (25th–75th Percentile):
480–610

ACT Composite Range (25th–75th Percentile):
22–29

ACT English Range (25th–75th Percentile):
22–29

ACT Math Range (25th–75th Percentile):
21–29

ACT Writing Range (25th–75th Percentile):
7–9

Top 10% of High School Class:
31%

Application Fee:
$30

Common Application Accepted?
Yes

Admissions E-Mail:
undergrad.admissions@valpo.edu

Admissions Web Site:
www.valpo.edu/admissions/

Early Action Deadline:
November 1

Early Action Notification:
December 1

Regular Decision Deadline:
January 15

Regular Decision Notification:
Rolling

Must-Reply-By Date:
May 1

Financial Information

Out-of-State Tuition:
$28,320

Room and Board:
$7,960

Books and Supplies:
$1,200

Average Amount of Federal Grant Aid:
$5,416

Percentage of Students Who Received Federal Grant Aid:
19%

Average Amount of Institution Grant Aid:
$11,287

Percentage of Students Who Received Institution Grant Aid:
96%

Average Amount of State Grant Aid:
$4,661

Percentage of Students Who Received State Grant Aid:
23%

Average Amount of Student Loans:
$6,982

Percentage of Students Who Received Student Loans:
64%

Total Need-Based Package:
$24,061

Percentage of Students Who Received Any Aid:
98%

Financial Aid Forms Deadline:
March 1

Financial Aid E-Mail:
finaid@valpo.edu

Financial Aid Web Site:
www.valpo.edu/finaid/

Academics

The Lowdown On...
Academics

Degrees Awarded
Associate degree
Bachelor's degree
Certificate
Master's degree
Post-bachelor's certificate
Post-master's certificate

Most Popular Majors
Law
Psychology
Registered Nursing (RN)
Sport and Fitness Management

Majors Offered
Arts
Biological Sciences
Business
Communications
Computer and Sciences
Education
Engineering
Environmental Sciences
Health Care
Languages and Literature
Law
Mathematics & Statistics
Philosophy and Religion
Physical Sciences

Psychology & Counseling
Recreation & Fitness
Social Sciences & Liberal Arts
Social Services

Undergraduate Schools/Divisions
College of Arts and Sciences
College of Business
College of Engineering
College of Nursing

Full-Time Instructional Faculty
242

Part-Time Instructional Faculty
115

Faculty with Terminal Degree
73%

Average Faculty Salary
$70,097

Student-Faculty Ratio
14:1

Class Sizes
Fewer than 20 students: 44%
20 to 49 students: 51%
50 or more students: 5%

Full-Time Retention Rate
85%

Part-Time Retention Rate
50%

Graduation Rate
75%

Remedial Services?
Yes

Academic/Career Counseling?
Yes

Instructional Programs
Occupational: Yes
Academic: Yes
Continuing Professional: Yes
Recreational/Avocational: Yes
Adult Basic Remedial: No
Secondary (High School): No

Special Credit Opportunities
Advanced Placement (AP) Credits: No
Dual Credit: Yes
Life Experience Credits: No

Special Study Options
Distance learning opportunities

Study abroad
Teacher certification (below the postsecondary level)

Other Academic Offerings

Accelerated program
Cooperative education program
Cross-registration
Double major
English as a Second Language (ESL)
Exchange student program (domestic)
Honors program
Independent study
Internships
Liberal arts/career combination
Student-designed major

Graduation Requirements

Cultural Diversity
Foreign languages
Humanities
Quantitative Analysis
Sciences (biological or physical)
Social science
Theology
Valpo Core

Best Places to Study
Christ College Commons
Christopher Center for Library and Information Resources

Did You Know?

In 2004, Valpo received its Phi Beta Kappa Charter, joining universities around the nation in the prestige and tradition of this academic honor society.

If you don't want to stick around for summer sessions but need to catch up on your credits, take an online class. Valpo offers several online courses in the summer (as well as a few during the academic year).

To fuel your mind, you need to feed your body! Valpo profs understand this, so twice a year during final exams, the Valpo profs serve Midnight Brunch in the Union. Just make a donation of canned goods or a dollar to charity, and you will get served by your profs.

The College of Engineering is the only designated engineering college at a Lutheran University in the United States. It also is ranked in the top 10th percentile in the nation.

Students Speak Out On...
Academics

Q Political Science Opportunities Readily Available
Our political science department is diverse and has a number of different fields to go into. We have a study abroad opportunity in which you can go to the American University in Washington D.C. We also have internship opportunities in D.C. through the Lutheran Consortium Program.

Q Extra Help - Willing to Work With You
One thing I found out about Valparaiso is all the professors are more than willing to work with you to give you extra help. They also are extremely understanding of your busy lives and if you need it they are usually willing to give you an extension on a project. I've found most of my professors to be personable, and all around fun to talk to!

Q English program is strong
The English program pushes you to become knowledgeable about all aspects of the English language, literature, and technologies. Classes range from grammar and composition to literature and criticism to the new technologies of writing. The professors are very welcoming to students and eager to help and are also very knowledgeable about their subject. Also, most of the English professors are currently publishing.

Q Professors Usually Available
Professors are almost always available when you need it. They give out cell phone numbers and have office hours that they must be available for students. Usually helpful. Quick to email back.

You Are More Than Just a Number
At Valpo, the class sizes are so small that you develop a great relationship with your professor and he/she truly cares about you and wants you to exceed in his/her class so they will help you with whatever you need.

Class sizes smaller than expected
A lot of the class sizes are a lot smaller than I expected, and most professors I have encountered are very willing to give students help.

Art program alright but small
The program here is alright but kind of small. You usually have to take class in a lot of different mediums, rather than majoring in just one. Some of the classes can be hard to get into because a lot of people take them as electives.

Plus and Minus
Great courses but some most of the prof's are not too good. I feel as if some know what they're talking about, however, they do a poor job in teaching that to us.

The College Prowler Take On...
Academics

All professors at VU are incredibly approachable. If you have an issue with the class, or even if you have a question about something else in the department, they are always open to talking with you. Each professor has posted office hours, but most are around outside of their office hours with their doors open. Some will even give out their cell phone numbers and encourage students to call them at home if they need help. Because the average class size at VU is very small, each of the professors will manage to learn who you are both in and out of class. They know if you don't show up to class, but if they mention it to you, it is because they want you to be able to make the most out of your time at VU. This helps a lot when writing recommendations since they actually know enough about you to write a unique letter.

Something unique about Valpo is that every class is taught by a professor rather than a graduate student or teacher's assistant. Very few classes even have TAs; science labs often have lab assistants, but when it comes to the actual classes, you can expect to see a professor standing at the front of the room lecturing and answering questions. VU is what many call a teaching school, and while the professors are strongly encouraged to do research and publish in journals, their primary focus and objective is to teach students. While some professors may not be the most personable, on the whole, they are accessible and ready to help you learn.

The College Prowler® Grade on
Academics: B-

A high Academics grade generally indicates that professors are knowledgeable, accessible, and genuinely interested in their students' welfare. Other determining factors include class size, how well professors communicate, and whether or not classes are engaging.

Local Atmosphere

The Lowdown On...
Local Atmosphere

City, State
Valparaiso, IN

Setting
Suburban

Distances to Nearest Major Cities
Chicago – IL – 1 hour
Indianapolis – IN – 2 hours, 30 minutes

Points of Interest
Chicago Street Theater
Hoosier Bat Factory
Indiana Dunes National Lakeshore
Memorial Opera House
Popcorn Festival
Porter County Fair
Wizard of Oz Fest

Shopping Centers
Downtown Valparaiso
Lighthouse Place Premium

Outlets
Southlake Mall
Valparaiso Marketplace

Major Sports Teams
Chicago Bears: NFL
Chicago Blackhawks: NHL
Chicago Bulls: NBA
Chicago Cubs: MLB
Chicago Fire: Soccer
Chicago Rush: Arena football
Chicago Storm: Indoor soccer
Chicago White Sox: MLB
Chicago Wolves: Hockey
Gary Railcats: Baseball
Gary Steelheads: Basketball

Movie Theaters

49'er Drive-In
675 N. Calumet Ave.
Valparaiso
(219) 462-6122

AMC Theaters Southlake Mall
2475 Southlake Mall
Merrillville
(219) 738-2652

Loews Cineplex
2350 E 79th Ave.
Merrillville
(219) 947-4072

Valparaiso County Seat 6
2849 Calumet Bell Park
Valparaiso
(219) 548-8788

Did You Know?

Fun Facts about Valparaiso:

- Birthplace of Orville Redenbacher.
- Author Don DeLillo wrote a play about a man's trip to the town titled Valparaiso.
- It was named after Valparaiso, Chile, by sailors who had served with Captain David Porter, an area native, in the War of 1812.
- It is nicknamed "Indiana's Vale of Paradise."
- In 1859, what is now Valparaiso University was founded as the Valparaiso Male and Female College, one of the first coed colleges in the country.

Local Slang:

- The Beach – Indiana Dunes
- The Bypass – Highway 49
- The City/Downtown – Chicago
- The Lake – Lake Michigan
- Pop – Carbonated beverages
- The Shot – Bryce Drew's game-winning three-point shot at the buzzer of the 1998 NCAA basketball tournament that took the Crusaders to their first-ever Sweet Sixteen appearance. Truly the stuff legends are made of—catch it on ESPN during any NCAA basketball tournament. There are endless replays.
- The Train – South Shore Line commuter train into Chicago
- Valpo – Slang for Valparaiso

Students Speak Out On...
Local Atmosphere

Q Valpo Campus
The school is beautiful. I live in Chicago and it is a very different atmosphere from there to Valpo. I love it.

Q Small Town College Experience
Valparaiso is a small town with not too many things to do locally, but there are a lot of activities on campus. It's a very safe atmosphere with more diversity than you might expect, as well as there being a religious presence.

Q Nothing Special.
Valpo is a good sized town, but there's not much excitement or things to do outside of drinking at fraternity parties. There are some good restaurants and a movie theater within close distance.

Q Valpo Atmosphere
Local atmosphere is that of a small town with a bustling downtown area that boasts a wide variety of restaurants that offers great outdoor dining combined with an array of small boutiques and small privaetly owned shops that a great selection of items. Culturally speaking it has a way to go and is not diverse. However it's a very safe place with a wide range of shopping opportunities and a healthy lifestyle is a priority. Attitudes toward college students is positive.

Q Family Town
if you are looking for a college town with a lot of night life, Valpo is not for you. But there are lots of restaurants and some shopping in the area, enough to get by. The Indiana Dunes are nearby which are a great attraction

Valpo Not Much of a College Town, but Chicago Close by

Valparaiso is a smaller city and does not stay open for typical college student hours. Most places close at 10pm, and only a handful are open until 3am. Steak and Shake is the best bet open 24 hours. However, Chicago is really close and really affordable to go to. There are a lot of opportunities there to engage in. It is also cheap with South Shore Line so nearby- only $6 each way.

Downtown Valpo

Within walking distance of campus, downtown Valpo has coffee shops that allow student musicians to make appearances and other great dining location for students. Beyond downtown, there isn't much more for students.

Cute but Sometimes Boring

The town offers a fair amount of activities throughout the year along with restaurants. There are a lot of volunteer opportunities. It can get old very fast though, especially if you are used to a bigger town with more things to do. It is only like an hour from Chicago however, if you are willing to take the trip.

The College Prowler Take On...
Local Atmosphere

Valparaiso is not a big city, and it never will be. It is very much like the kind of midwestern town you see in the movies. There is a nice downtown area that has a lot of small coffee shops and specialty stores, however the shopping mall that most students go to is in Merrillville, 20 minutes down the road. Valpo's downtown may only keep you busy for a little while, but visiting some of those shops just once doesn't do them justice as they beg to have you wander through them again and again. Also, Valpo has quite a few restaurants that are fun to eat at every once in awhile.

In the beginning of the year, the city celebrates the Popcorn Festival in which the streets are closed off so vendors can set up tents everywhere. There is a variety of food and gifts that can be bought, and it is a great way to get to know new people since it is within the first few weeks of school. If there is anything you do not find in Valpo, Merrillville is the next best bet up the road. A little further away is the big city life of Chicago.

Whether by car or by train, it takes a little over an hour to get into the Windy City. Chicago has everything you could possibly think of with sports teams, concerts, theaters, museums, and shopping. Visiting the city never gets old, and many students will go for the day or indulge in a weekend in the city. Union Board offers many events and trips into the city as well. Valpo is the perfect place to have a small town feel while going to school, but the bigger city with more exciting nightlife is not terribly far down the road.

The College Prowler® Grade on
Local Atmosphere: C

A high Local Atmosphere grade indicates that the area surrounding campus is safe and scenic. Other factors include nearby attractions, proximity to other schools, and the town's attitude toward students.

Health & Safety

The Lowdown On...
Health & Safety

Security Office
VU Police Department
816 Union St.
(219) 464-5430 (non-emergency)
www.valpo.edu/vupd

Safety Services
Bike registration
Emergency call-box phones
Student escort service

Crimes on Campus
Aggravated Assault: 0
Arson: 0
Burglary: 21
Murder/Manslaughter: 0
Robbery: 0
Sex Offenses: 5
Vehicle Theft: 0

Health Center
Student Health Center
1406 LaPorte Ave.
(219) 464-5060

www.valpo.edu/healthcenter
Monday–Friday 8 a.m.–4:30 p.m.

Health Services
Allergy shots
Basic medical care
Counseling services
Flu shots
Immunizations
Lab services
Medical referrals
Physicals
STD testing
Wellness exams
Women's health

Day Care Services?
No

Did You Know?

The VU Police Department often teams up with fraternities, sororities, and other campus groups to provide informational and instructional seminars related to self-defense, drug prevention, alcohol abuse, and other related topics.

Students Speak Out On...
Health & Safety

Q I feel very safe
I feel very safe on all parts of campus.

Q It's So Safe It's Boring.
The worst things that happen at Valpo are usually people getting busted in the dorms with alcohol or something. It's a very safe and friendly environment.

Q Insanely Safe
The way the campus is set up, unless you're walking from the union to the semi-off campus apts or the frat houses, you're completely safe. Nothing bad can happen, it seems. There are red emergency buttons placed everywhere, on-campus security, and lots of other people, mostly good ones.

Q Campus Is Very Safe
Crime is very low on campus. One rarely hears of any sort of crime. Cops have a strong presence in and around campus. They are on constant patrol.

Q Safe Campus
I have never felt unsafe on Valpo's campus. It's small and beautiful. Lock doors at night to avoid petty theft. VUPD can be a little over-reactive toward drinking policy though.

Q Police Always Around and Usually Helpful
The police are on duty with two officers 24 hours a day. Sometimes they get a little excessive, but overall they are not a burden. They are there to protect you and will only stop you if they feel that something is up.

Very Safe Campus

Overall, I feel very safe not just on the campus but as I walk through town. I believe that Valpo as a school does a fine job ensuring are safety and I feel very comfortable even when it is dark at night.

Campus Is Overally Safe

Campus police act phyco and try to enforce rules too hard. Which could be a good thing becuase it makes the campus safe.

The College Prowler Take On...
Health & Safety

Quite simply, safety's not an issue. It may be uncomfortable to walk alone on the paths from the main library back to the dorms, but it's definitely safe. Very few incidents have occurred on or around campus in the past few years. Even with those couple of incidents, the vast majority of the student body have no problem walking around campus late into the night hours. If walking doesn't seem like a good option, the Student Escort Service (or LAID Van) is up and running from 6 p.m.–2 a.m. every night, carting students all around campus. On the weekends, the van even runs down to the fraternity houses, so you can make it to the fraternity parties and back with minimal work on your part.

VUPD makes themselves pretty visible on campus. They always have two vehicles patrolling campus to make sure nothing is awry. They are around for the students' safety, and it is evident that the majority of the students feel safe on campus. The police officers most often catch people for drinking or for parking in the wrong area, rather than any criminal activity. If there is any crime on campus, President Heckler makes sure that all students get an email about it right away to explain the situation.

You can wander outside of campus in the evenings with little concern, but just always be aware of yourself and your belongings. Valpo is safe, but just like everywhere else, it is a good idea to keep track of your stuff—if you don't, someone else probably will.

The College Prowler® Grade on
Health & Safety: B

A high grade in Health & Safety means that students generally feel safe, campus police are visible, blue-light phones and escort services are readily available, and safety precautions are not overly necessary.

Computers

The Lowdown On...
Computers

Wireless Access
Yes: Available in the Christopher Center, dorms, and in most academic buildings

24-Hour Labs?
Yes: Union and residence halls

Charged to Print?
Yes: Students are alloted 300 pages per semester but can have additions made by professors. If they exceed the allotted amount, they must pay for extra pages ($5 per 100 pages)

Special Software & Hardware Discounts
None

Did You Know?

Like to waste paper? The infamous orientation story about what not to print includes the entire script for Monty Python and the Holy Grail. Try to avoid printing scripts for movies that you already know by heart.

If you are in the Union's 24-hour computer lab after 2 a.m. when the Student Escort Service stops, you can call VUPD for a ride back to your dorm.

No more lines! Valpo has adopted online registration for classes so you don't have to wait in the throngs of students at the Registrar's Office—you don't even have to be wearing pants when you register for classes.

Students Speak Out On...
Computers

Q Great Computer Availability
There are a TON of computers at Valpo. All of the computers are up to date and there are many and varied locations for labs on campus. Near midterms or finals, it can sometimes get a little crowded, but there is always a computer to be found. Also, the vast majority of campus has Wifi access to the internet, so you can use your own computer essentially everywhere.

Q Very Good
Highly available and extremely fast all over campus. The exceptions are the Sun Microsystems ones in the Weather Center, but those are supposedly being gotten rid of soon.

Q Computers Always Available
There are computer labs in every dorm and in the library and union. The union and dorm labs are accessible 24 hours a day. Sometimes a little slow but always available. It is still nice to have your own computer. Wifi is in every dorm and most academic buildings.

Q Overall, they're good
They have their problems from time to time, but overall they get the job done.

Q Some Labs Are Not up to Date
While most of the computers and labs are up to date, there are others that still run very slow and are still in 2003. It is more difficult to do homework when some computers do not have the software or software that is up to date.

Decent, Not Great
Printing is a pain, so bring your own printer (scanner not necessary). Wireless internet is terrible in some rooms, but fine in others, but there are ports for ethernet cords available. More of the campus should have wireless internet access.

Computers can be improved
Frankly, the wireless network at Valparaiso leaves much to be desired as most students can not obtain quality Internet access from their dorm rooms. Labs that are located within each dorm building are not well maintained and often run out of paper or ink for printing. Overall, I think this would be an area where Valpo can make large improvements.

Come Computers Are Great, Others Are Archaic
The computers in the dorms are awful. They are super slow and work questionably at best. If you go to the library or union they work fine, but everywhere else they don't work very well.

The College Prowler Take On...
Computers

Computers are just a part of everyday modernism that has spilled over into college life. VU is no exception to this rule. Each dorm room has a space for two desktop computers to be plugged into the network. The majority of students bring lap tops that rely on wireless Internet, though. Not that you need to bring a computer to survive on this campus, but most students bring their own simply because it is more convenient.

There are plenty of computers and computer labs on campus, considering that each dorm maintains a lab of its own. You won't find any problems getting a computer, except of course during finals week when everyone on campus is working on finals projects and papers. The only downside to the individual labs in the dorms is that the computers are usually about two to three years older than the one sitting on the desk in your room. Some of them are in desperate need of updates, but the new ones in the library and Union are great to use.

The College Prowler® Grade on Computers: B-

A high grade in Computers designates that computer labs are available, the computer network is easily accessible, and the campus's computing technology is up-to-date.

Facilities

The Lowdown On...
Facilities

Campus Size
320 acres

Student Centers
Harre Union

Main Libraries
Christopher Center Library

Service & Maintenance Staff
218

Popular Places to Chill
Games and Rec Center
Grinders in Christopher Center Library

Bar on Campus
None

Bowling on Campus
None

Coffeehouse on Campus
Grinders in the Christopher Center
Perks in the Harre Union

Movie Theater on Campus
None

Favorite Things To Do
Valpo has a wealth of activities and events to attend. The VUCA (Center for the Arts) is home to plays, concerts, recitals, and lectures, as well as the University's Brauer Museum of Art. The Brauer Museum is home to many modern American artworks, including pieces by Georgia O'Keefe. Recitals and concerts of various campus music ensembles and groups also take place in the Chapel of the Resurrection. Various lectures, debates, and the Christ College Symposium Series take place in the Mueller Hall Refectory. Lectures and films are conducted in the Neils Science Center auditorium. Poetry slams and book discussions, as well as small concerts, often pop up in the Café at the Union. In addition, departmental or special-interest lectures often take place in the academic buildings around campus, as well as in the Lumina Room of Huegli Hall. Athletic events take place at the ARC (Athletics Recreation Center), Brown Field (football field), the new softball diamond, Eastgate (soccer field), and the Emory Bauer Baseball Field.

Did You Know?

 The cement structure outside of the Christopher Center Library actually breaks up enough sunlight so that the floor-to-ceiling windows do not cause increased aging of the books.

Students Speak Out On...
Facilities

Q Library is so nice
I absolutely love the library. I appreciate the quiet floors, but also that there is a space for talking and fun. I love Grinders, and the windows are just fantastic. In the nice weather, my friends and I sit out on the terrace and it's just great.

Q Harre Union
The new union is great, but there should still be more food options and places to eat around campus.

Q New Library and Union, Beautiful Chapel
The major buildings on campus (library, union, chapel, VUCA) are beautiful. Dorms are okay and most academic buildings are older, but they still have character beauty. The ARC has horrible hours, but with the new rec center it might be better.

Q Christopher Center
the facilities are very clean, and very comfortable

Q Overall Good
The new buildings are awesome. Very modern and, well, new. The have very clean areas and excellent air conditioning. Some buildings, however, have been around for a few too many decades, like Meier and the Christ College buildings that are old and dungeon-like.

💬 The Library Is Really Helpful

The library just opened in 2004 and is well equipped with a multitude of resources. Four floors of floor to ceiling windows. Really spacious so you don't feel like you are stuck in the library. ASRS makes finding materials easy.

💬 Things are being updated

The buildings are pretty old and outdated, but they offer a sort of old-fashioned charm to the campus. The university is also working on updating everything.

💬 Facilities Need Improvement

While the facilities at VU are sufficient, the lack of modernity can inhibit higher degrees of learning. The newest buildings - Union, Library, Kallay-Christopher - are excellent buildings that serve their purposes well. However, the majority of other buildings severely lack in their abilities to teach at the highest degree.

The College Prowler Take On...
Facilities

Valpo has been updating the campus over the last few years with some really nice renovations and new facilities, including the library, Union, and fitness center. The library is a great addition to campus. It brings a state-of-the-art facility to a campus that is trying to move forward and expand. The spacious atmosphere and floor-to-ceiling windows promotes a relaxed setting to study in. The Harre Union opened in January of 2009 and has a games and recreation center, meeting rooms, lounges, a 24-hour computer lab, and a ballroom that hosts numerous events. It has two different eating places: one that is available at meal times and another open later into the night. The facility has become a center for student life since many activities are held there on a weekly basis.

The ARC, while nice in size, is usually overrun with athletic teams and their practices. However, the recent addition of the fitness center offers a wide range of options for non-varsity athletes. It is state-of-the-art with a cardio area that has 25 machines, a weight training area, and an aerobics area. There are also fitness classes available. The facility is free for students and is open much longer than the old gym was. It makes exercising accessible for students so they can fight off the freshman fifteen with ease.

The VUCA (Center for the Arts) and Kallay-Christopher are also newer buildings serving academic purposes. Both are equipped with up-to-date classrooms and equipment. The VUCA also has a museum, theater, and recital hall that hosts many events and performances throughout the year.

The College Prowler® Grade on
Facilities: B-

A high Facilities grade indicates that the campus is aesthetically pleasing and well-maintained; facilities are state-of-the-art, and libraries are exceptional. Other determining factors include the quality of both athletic and student centers and an abundance of things to do on campus.

Campus Dining

The Lowdown On...
Campus Dining

Average Meal Plan Cost
$3050 per year

Freshman Meal Plan Required?
Yes

24-Hour Dining
None

Dining Halls & Campus Restaurants

Campus Café

Location: Harre Union
Food: Breakfast, lunch, and dinner served cafeteria-style
Hours: Monday–Thursday 7:30 a.m.–11 p.m., Friday 7:30 a.m.–12 a.m., Saturday 11 a.m.–12 a.m., Sunday 2 p.m.–11 p.m.

Founders Table

Location: Harre Union
Food: Entrees, pizza, salad, stir-fry
Hours: Monday–Saturday 7 a.m.–2 p.m., 4:30 p.m.–8 p.m., Sunday 9 a.m.–2 p.m., 4:30 p.m.–8 p.m.

Grinders

Location: Christopher Center
Food: Sandwiches, snacks, coffee
Hours: Monday–Thursday 9:30 a.m.–11 p.m., Friday 9:30 a.m.–2 p.m., Sunday 7 p.m.–11 p.m.

Student Favorites: Campus Dining Hall

Founder's Table

Student Favorites: Breakfast Food on Campus

Sunday Waffles at the Union

Student Favorites: Lunch/Dinner Entrée on Campus

Paninis at the Sizzle in the Founder's Table

Student Favorites: Late-night Snack on Campus

Coffee from Grinders
Ice Cream or Smoothie at Freshens

Off-Campus Places to Use Flex Money

None

Did You Know?

Dining Services posts the nutrition information for all main-line menu items.

If you're left with tons of meal card money at the end of the semester, you can donate it to the food pantry. Only $150 will transfer from fall semester to spring semester.

Students Speak Out On...
Campus Dining

Q Adult Scholar
As an adult scholar I don't get to utilize dining services too much. However the new Union has is the main gathering place for meals. Besides the beauty of this new building thge menus are pretty good offering brick oven pizza, a fresh deli sandwich section, a hot meal section topped off with a great salad and desert bar.There are great salads and sandwiches pre-packed along with a great variety of fresh fruit, soy products and soda

Q Meal Options on Campus in Two Places
There's only two main places to grab food on campus, but they do have a variety of options. There's an executive chef now that makes something new every day… although the schedule does rotate. Every once in a while there will be a day dedicated to a food like corn and everything will have it in it. There are no fast food choices or highly known brand names on campus.

Q Food Is Good!
Having experienced Valpo's old Union food, the new Harre Union improves the dining options by 200%. Many different kinds of food are available throughout the week, and for the most part food is prepared while you watch, so you know it's fresh. Sometimes vegetarian or other healthier options are not as prevalent -- your best option is a salad (which can be pretty expensive).

Q Yummy but Crowded
lots of variety and good quality food, meal times can get really crowded thought and it takes forever to pay

Q Campus Food

The campus food selection is good. Their is a variety of healthy choices, an availability of vegetarian options, and fresh fruits and vegetables. However, sometimes the menu is repetitive, but lately the entrees have been more adventurous.

Q Good Enough for This College Student

It's not the best, but I'm pretty easy to please. I love that I can always make a sandwich or salad, and there is usually a pretty good variety of choices for the main course. Waffles on Sunday mornings are the best- I still come from off campus for them.

Q Same Items

I wish there was a better late night option. There are a lot of wonderful grab-n'-go items and great sit-down items, but sometimes it seems as though it's the same choices every week or two.

Q Lack of Options

-only 2 places to get food-limited hours of business-not much variety-poor quality

The College Prowler Take On...
Campus Dining

Campus food is better than most high school cafeteria food. The meal card is like a debit card system because you pay for what you buy. There is no "pay for two meals a day" option. This way students can come in any time of the day and grab whatever they need. For food, the new Harre Union offers more choices with a café-style facility at one end and a sit-down meal area at the other. The latter (Founder's Table) has an executive chef and three other main menu options. There is always a vegetarian option, and the food is made in front of you most of the time. Salad, sandwich, and soup bars are always popular, but there is also typical college food like hamburgers, grilled cheese, etc., along with brick oven pizza, paninis, pasta, and the chef's creation.

Dining Services manages to do a pretty good job feeding the entire campus some decent food. Setting up a menu to feed 2,000 students that includes variety and choices, yet tries to maintain a certain nutritional standard, can't be easy.

Theme nights are favorite occasions for many students. Different foods will be featured at different times of year in almost every dish. There was corn night, apple night, and duck night, to name a few. The space is decorated to fit the theme, and even the cafeteria ladies dress up in Afro-wigs or sombreros, depending on the event. A lot of students even get to know some of the cafeteria ladies. They smile and greet you whether you are sleepily stopping by for a doughnut and juice before trudging to class or sitting down with a group of friends for dinner.

The College Prowler® Grade on Campus Dining

The grade on Campus Dining addresses the quality of both school-owned dining halls and independent on-campus restaurants as well as the price, availability, and variety of food.

Off-Campus Dining

The Lowdown On...
Off-Campus Dining

Restaurant Listings

Applebee's
Food: American
670 Morthland Dr.
(219) 477-3868
www.applebees.com
Price: $8–$15

Arby's
Food: Fast food
2101 Calumet Ave.
(219) 464-4147
www.arbys.com
Price: $2–$8

Billy Jack's Café & Grill
Food: Californian, Southwestern, Italian, Mediterranean
2904 Calumet Ave.
(219) 477-3797
Price: $10–$20
Cool Features: For $24.95, you can pick up dinner for 4 to go.

Bistro 157
Food: Gourmet
157 Lincolnway
(219) 462-0992

Price: $15–$50
Cool Features: Very upscale, and very expensive.

Bob Evans
Food: Diner
2201 E. Morthland Dr.
(219) 464-9201
www.bobevans.com
Price: $5–$10
Cool Features: New menu items all the time.

Broadway Café & Ice Cream Parlor
Food: American, Greek, Italian
1805 Morthland Ave. (U.S. 30)
(219) 464-0112
Price: $5–$10
Cool Features: Great ice cream!

BuffaLouie's
Food: Wings, salads, sandwiches
3300 Calumet Ave.
(219) 462-1717
www.buffalouies.com
Price: $20–$50
Cool Features: Restaurant decorated with Valpo athletic gear.

Café Paradiso
Food: Northern Italian
21 Linconway
(219) 476-0099
Price: $10–$15
Cool Features: Chef/owner from Rome—all meals are authentic Italian.

Chili's Grill & Bar
Food: American
250 Silhavy Rd.
(219) 465-7344
www.chilis.com
Price: $8–$15

China House
Food: Chinese
120 E. Lincolnway
(219) 462-5788
Cool Features: Part of old downtown Valparaiso, China House is quite authentic.

Designer Desserts
Food: Baked goods
56 E. Lincolnway
(219) 465-0008
designerdessertsbakery.com

Dish Restaurant
Food: American
3907 N. Calumet Ave.
(219) 465-9221
Price: $10–$25
Cool Features: Urban dining in a small-town setting.

Domino's Pizza
Food: Pizza
1707 La Porte Ave.
(219) 465-5500
www.dominos.com
Price: $3–$8

Don Quijote
Food: Spanish
119 E. Lincoln Way
(219) 462-7976
www.donquijoterestaurant-in.com
Price: $8–$25
Cool Features: Only authentic Spanish in Indiana.

El Amigo Mexican Restaurant
Food: Mexican
3032 N. Calumet Ave.
(219) 531-5606
Price: $3–$7
Cool Features: Late-night favorite for Valpo students.

El Charro
Food: Mexican
807 E. Lincoln Way
(219) 548-3703

El Salto
Food: Mexican
3304 Calument Ave.
(219) 462-0100
Price: $10–$15
Cool Features: Giant margaritas!

The Evelyn Bay Coffee Company
Food: Coffee
3800 Calumet Ave.
(219) 510-5802
asipabove.com

Gelsosomo's Pizza
Food: Pizza and Italian
2605 La Porte Ave.
(219) 477-4255
Price: $10–$25
Cool Features: Great place to enjoy pizza as a sit-down dinner.

Hungry Howie's Pizza
Food: Pizza
15 Roosevelt Rd.
(219) 476-0800
hungryhowies.com

Jade Garden
Food: Chinese
3022 N. Calumet Ave.
(219) 464-9860
Price: $10–$15
Cool Features: Jade Garden delivers to VU dorms.

Jimmy's Café
55 Michigan Ave.
(219) 462-9167

Johnnies Round the Clock Restaurant
217 E. Lincoln Way
(219) 462-6339
www.roundtheclock.com
Price: $8–$15
Cool Features: Dinner and lunch specials.

Kelsey's Steak House
Food: Steak, seafood
1905 Morthland Ave. (U.S. 30)
(219) 465-4022
Price: $10–$25
Cool Features: There's a giant steer out front.

Maria Elena's
Food: American, Italian, Mexican
454 S. Greenwich
(219) 477-2490
Price: $10–$15
Cool Features: A romantic place for a date if you lack transportation—very close to campus!

Martini's
Food: Steak, seafood
1004 Calumet Ave.
(219) 464-0801
Price: $10–$25
Cool Features: VU Jazz Lab provides live music regularly.

Mia Cucina
Food: Italian, sports bar
210 Aberdeen Dr.
(219) 548-3300
Price: $8–$15
Cool Features: Good drink specials (Tuesdays 10-beer buckets for $10).

Noodles and Company 510
Food: Asian, Mediterranean
71 Silhavy Rd,
(219) 548-0921

Pastimes
Food: American
175 Lincolnway
(219) 462-3786
Price: $5–$10
Cool Features: Full bar.

Pesto's Italian Restaurant & Pizzeria
Food: Italian, pizza
3123 Calumet Ave.
(219) 462-0993
Price: $10–$20
Cool Features: Looks like a real Italian bistro, complete with balcony.

Pikk's Tavern
Food: Steak, sandwiches
62 E. Lincoln Way
(219) 476-7455
pikkstavern.com

Steak 'n Shake
Food: Fast food
1251 Strongbow Center Dr.
(800) 357-8768
www.steaknshake.com
Price: $5–$10

Strongbow Inn
Food: Turkey, fresh bakery
1251 Strongbow Center Dr.
(U.S. 30)
(219) 462-5121
Price: $10–$30
Cool Features: Strongbow has the best rolls in the world and an awesome buffet on Wednesdays.

Subway
Food: Subs, salad, soup
3004 Calumet Ave.
(219) 462-9666
www.subway.com
Price: $3–$8

Suzie's Café & Catering
Food: Homemade bread, cinnamon rolls, soup, sandwiches
1050 South Point Dr.
(219) 462-5500
Price: $5–$10

Viking Chili Bowl
Food: Chili, breakfast
105 Morthland Ave. (U.S. 30)
(219) 462-0800
Price: $5–$10

Best Asian
Dynasty Buffet
Jade Garden

Best Breakfast
Bob Evans Restaurant
Broadway Café
Jimmy's Café
Viking Chili Bowl

Best Coffee
Designer Desserts
Evelyns Bay Coffee Company
Starbucks

Best Dessert
Designer Desserts

Best Healthy
Noodles and Company 510
Subway

Best Late-Night
El Amigo
Jimmy John's
Steak 'n Shake

Best Mexican
El Amigo
El Charro
El Salto

Best Pizza
Domino's (best for your wallet)
Gelsosomo's (best taste)
Greeks Pizzeria
Hungry Howie's

Best Wings
Buffalo Wild Wings
BuffaLouie's
Wings, Etc.

Best Place to Take a Date
Maria Elena's

Best Place to Take Your Parents
Kelsey's Steakhouse
Pikk's Tavern

24-Hour Dining
Arby's
Johnnies Round the Clock
Steak 'n Shake

Other Places to Check Out
Buffalo Wild Wings
Denny's
Dynasty Buffet
Greek's Pizzeria
Jimmy John's
King Gyros
Panera Bread
Quiznos
Starbucks
Taco Bell
Tony's Place
Wings, etc.

Grocery Stores
Town and Country Market
1605 Calumet Ave.
(219) 464-8606

Wal-Mart SuperCenter
2400 E Morthland Dr.
(219) 465-2799

WiseWay
2800 Calumet Ave.
(219) 464-3571

Did You Know?

Valparaiso is home to the Popcorn Festival in honor of Orville Redenbacher, a Valpo native.

Want to eat healthy? A Natural Ovens Bakery (3400 Mariposa; www.naturalovens.com) is located in Valparaiso, and their products are available at area grocery stores. In addition, Au Naturel (1708 Lincolnway) is an organic and health food market, and it's now within walking distance of campus.

Students Speak Out On...
Off-Campus Dining

Q Jimmy Johns
Super fast and friendly. Plus a filling meal for $5.

Q Good Variety
It's a college town so there's plenty of pizza and fast food. But there are also a few good restaurants. I recommend Jimmy's Cafe! It's a few blocks west of campus and great for breakfast at 5am for all the real partiers that can last past 2am.

Q Food Is Valpo's Specialty
There are tons of good restaurants in town. There are a few good cheap restaurants that are good for students (Broadway, Viking Chili Bowl, Around the Clock, King Gyros) cheap Mexican places (El Amigo!). New Dragon has really good, fast Chinese. There are nicer restaurants too (The Dish, Don Quijote, Bistro 151). I don't know many towns this size that have 2 taco bells, 2 McDonalds, and 2 Burger Kings, but Valpo does.

Q A Nice Town :)
Cool cafes that I should visit more often before I graduate (Blackbird, etc.) Good fast food places somewhat nearby (Jimmy John's, Subway, Pizza places). There are also a few nice sit-down restaurants.

Q Many Off Campus Options
There are many off campus options close by that the V-Line can take you to. This includes Chilis, Red Robin, TGIFridays, Noodles, and Coldstone. There are some cute locally owned places that are pretty nice as well. There

are many more options 20 minutes down the road in Merrillville. They have more higher class options like Olive Garden and Joe's Crab Shack.

Q Valparaiso Eating

There is a lot of variety because the city is so close to Chicago. The cost is about average, and there are tons of locations around the campus so convenience is high.

Q Good Options, but I Don't Eat Off Campus

There are plenty of options off campus that are located fairly close. Jimmy John's, Subway, Dominos, Culvers, and Dairy Queen are located within 5 minutes of campus. Dominos even offers 1/2 priced Fridays! There are plenty of other restaurants located throughout town, but some/most require a car or long walk to get to.

Q It's Not Perfect, but It's Good.

There's a decent variety of restaurants within walking distance of campus. There's a couple pizza chains (Hungry Howie's, Dominoes, Papa John's delivers), there are the usual chains, and there are some good restaurants nearby. The easiest place to reach is King Gyro, which has really reasonable prices and fairly good portions.

The College Prowler Take On...
Off-Campus Dining

What the town of Valparaiso lacks in exciting activities, it makes up for in dining. Valparaiso has an incredible blend of fast food, casual eats, and fancy dining options. Every fast food venue you can think of is available, including a Quizno's and Panera Bread, along with old favorites like Steak 'n Shake. Casual dining options like Applebee's and Chili's are available close to campus. Everything from Italian to Chinese to Spanish is waiting for your taste buds. Maria Elena's is a huge favorite of everyone on campus. They have American, Mexican, and Italian cuisine with prices comparable to Chili's. El Amigo, while not fancy in the least, is a late-night favorite. You'll need a car to get there, but from what everyone says, the burritos are worth more than the five-minute drive. There are many unique small restaurants in the city, too.

Dining hall options can quickly exhaust themselves despite the Dining Services' staff doing what they can to vary the menu and come up with new and exciting meals. It's easy to take an evening and head out with friends to one of the great restaurants in Valparaiso. The best thing is that once you've tried one place, you know you could always go back again, but with all the other options, why not try something new?

The College Prowler® Grade on
Off-Campus Dining: B-

A high Off-Campus Dining grade implies that off-campus restaurants are affordable, accessible, and worth visiting. Other factors include the variety of cuisine and the availability of alternative options (vegetarian, vegan, kosher).

Campus Housing

The Lowdown On...
Campus Housing

On-Campus Housing Available?
Yes

Campus Housing Capacity
2,021

Average Housing Costs
$4,910

Number of Dormitories
9

Number of Campus-Owned Apartments
1

Dormitories

807 Mound Street
Floors: 3
Number of Occupants: 100–249
Bathrooms: Communal
Coed: Yes
Residents: Upperclassmen
Room Types: Triples
Special Features: 24-hour computer lab, large kitchen, laundry facilities, study rooms

Alumni Hall
Floors: 5
Number of Occupants: 250–499
Bathrooms: Communal, some private
Coed: Yes
Residents: Freshmen, some upperclassmen
Room Types: Doubles
Special Features: First-floor rooms have private bathroom and are available to upperclass men; 24-hour computer lab, large study room, chapel, floor TV lounges, pool table, ping-pong table, large kitchen, laundry facilities, large TV lounge

Brandt Hall
Floors: 5
Number of Occupants: 250–499
Bathrooms: Communal, some private
Coed: Yes
Residents: Freshmen and upperclassmen
Room Types: Doubles
Special Features: First-floor rooms have private bathroom, many international students live in Brandt; 24-hour computer lab, attached cafeteria, large study room, chapel, floor TV lounges, pool table, ping-pong table, large kitchen, laundry facilities, large TV lounge

Guild Hall
Floors: 4
Number of Occupants: 250–499
Bathrooms: Communal
Coed: No, women only
Residents: All upperclassmen
Room Types: Singles, doubles, triples, quads
Special Features: A few select rooms include a bathroom, connected to Memorial Hall; air conditioning, 24-hour computer lab, private study rooms, chapel, ping-pong and foosball tables, laundry facilities, large TV lounge

Kade-Duesenberg German House
Floors: 4
Number of Occupants: <20
Bathrooms: Private
Coed: Yes
Residents: Upperclassmen
Room Types: Doubles

Special Features: Home to German studies students (must speak German at all times in the public areas of house), above the German Cultural Center; large kitchen, laundry facilities

Lankenau Hall
Floors: 5
Number of Occupants: 250–499
Bathrooms: Communal, some private
Coed: Yes
Residents: Freshmen, some upperclassmen
Room Types: Doubles
Special Features: First-floor rooms have movable furniture, private bathrooms available to upperclassman women; 24-hour computer lab, study rooms, chapel, floor TV lounges, fitness room (weight machines and treadmill), foosball and ping-pong tables, laundry facilities

Memorial Hall
Floors: 4
Number of Occupants: 250–499
Bathrooms: Communal, some private
Coed: Yes
Residents: Upperclassmen
Room Types: Singles, doubles, triples, quads
Special Features: Select rooms include bathroom, connected to Guild Hall (shares amenities with Guild Hall)

Scheele Hall
Floors: 5
Number of Occupants: 250–499
Bathrooms: Communal
Coed: No, women only
Residents: Upperclassmen
Room Types: Singles, doubles
Special Features: Most of this building is devoted to housing sororities; 24-hour computer lab, large study room, floor lounges and kitchens on second and third floor, chapel, laundry facilities

Wehrenberg Hall
Floors: 4
Number of Occupants: 250–499
Bathrooms: Communal
Coed: Yes
Residents: Upperclassmen
Room Types: Singles, doubles
Special Features: Air conditioning, attached cafeteria, 24-hour computer lab, conference room, floor lounges with kitchens, recreation room with pool and ping-pong tables, laundry facilities on each floor, large TV and piano lounge, study lounges

Campus-Owned Apartments
The Uptown East
Floors: 4
Bathrooms: Private
Coed: Yes
Room Types: Two-, three-, and four-bedroom apartments (singles)
Special Features: Amenities include computer lab, DVD theater, fitness center, game room, student lounges with free wireless access. Apartments are fully furnished and have 42-inch flat screen TVs in the living rooms, full-size beds, washer/dryer. Utilities are included.

Freshmen Living On Campus
88%

Undergrads Living On Campus
66%

Best Freshman Dorms
Alumni
Lankenau

Best Upperclassman Dorms
Guild/ Memorial
Uptown East Apartments
Wehrenberg

Worst Freshman Dorms
Brandt

Worst Upperclassman Dorms
Brandt
Scheele

Types of Housing Offered
Apartments for single students
Coed dorms
Fraternity/sorority housing
Theme housing
Women's dorms

What You Get
Bed
Bookshelf
Cable TV
Closet
Desk and chair
Ethernet access
Medicine cabinet
Phone
Sink
Window coverings

Available for Rent
MicroFridge

Also Available
Valpo has a special-interest religious house, the Christian Fellowship House.
Valpo offers international houses like the German House and the International Student House.

Did You Know?

Some dorms do not allow microwaves in the rooms unless it's a joint system with the refrigerator, but all floors are equipped with microwaves.

Bicycle racks are available outside each dorm.

Each floor in the freshman dorms has at least one RA per wing; upperclassman dorms often have fewer RAs.

Students Speak Out On...
Campus Housing

Q Campus Housing
The housing at Valpo is amazing. The rooms are spacious and classy.

Q Dorms aren't bad
Freshman dorms aren't horrible—they're better than most large state schools. Upperclassman dorms are a bit bigger.

Q Freshman halls are okay
Freshman halls are typical, and upperclassman options vary. The one for upperclassman women is the same as a freshman hall, so no upgrade there. The new apartments through the university are nice but very expensive.

Q Dorms Need Updates
The freshman dorms are all uniform so it doesn't really matter which building you're in. Students are required to live on campus until senior year so there are few options when you're a sophomore so many get stuck in Brandt or Scheele (sorority building). There is a new apartment/suite style housing that seems pretty nice. Stick with Guild/Memorial if you can...it's the most beautiful!

Q Residential Halls Could Use Improvement
The freshman dorms are stuck in the 1960's with not too many amenities. The closeness of residents make the community really strong; the buildings just need a pick me up. The upperclassmen dorms are nicer even though they are older. They have more room and more design options. Newly added Uptown East Apartments give a

lot of options on where to live. Sorority housing though is the same as freshmen dorms, which makes it hard to encourage people to live there.

Q Reasonable
Dorms were fine for me. A lot of other people complain about them. Fraternity housing varies. I love my Sigma Pi houses, but they're still run down pieces of crap.

Q A Variety of Dorms
The freshman dorms aren't the greatest, but it is very easy to make friends there. The Resident Assistants do a great job with social programs so you can meet new people. There are three options for the upperclassmen. You can either live in a building that has recently been updated or one of the oldest buildings on campus. Both are good in their own way, and it is whatever you prefer. There are also campus owned apartments right off of campus and they are extremely nice. You can have your own room and bathroom.

Q Valpo Dorms
Guild/Memorial halls are the best to live in. Residents have partial control over heating and air conditioning in rooms, spacious. Decent bathrooms.Wehrenberg hall has air conditioning, laundry rooms on each floor.Scheele, Brandt, Alumni, and Lankenau halls all have small rooms, the furniture is built in. Very warm in the winter. 807 Mound St. is a long walk from the center of campus, no air conditioning.Uptown East Apartments are available through University housing, full kitchen, fully furnished, 1 bathroom for each bedroom, Very expensive. Need at least JR. Standing to live here.Most Seniors live off campus.

The College Prowler Take On...
Campus Housing

Unless you are a commuter student, you have to have senior status to move off campus unless you join a fraternity that has housing. Being on campus does have benefits, however, including being closer to classes, and it is usually cheaper just to stay in the dorms. There are also laundry facilities available in each building, free access to the campus computer network and cable, and a housekeeping staff that cleans the bathrooms everyday. Everyone manages to find a dorm that they like the best. Some students love the noise and constant movement of the freshman dorms, so they grab the rooms (which have their own bathroom) on the first floor of those dorms. Other students move into 'Berg (Wehrenberg), Guild, or Memorial—all of which have been remodeled in the past 10 years. The new option of Uptown East Apartments provides University-owned apartments with the ability to have multiple roommates and amenities while staying on campus.

Overall, the residence halls are pretty nice. The rooms are decent—bigger than the matchboxes at state universities—but not as plush as you would expect from smaller institutions. Some students cannot wait to move off campus, but most find that the community built through staying on campus for at least three years makes a better college experience. The community at Valpo is definitely unique, and the way the residence halls are situated probably contributes to that fact.

The College Prowler® Grade on Campus Housing: B-

A high Campus Housing grade indicates that dorms are clean, well-maintained, and spacious. Other determining factors include variety of dorms, proximity to classes, and social atmosphere.

Off-Campus Housing

The Lowdown On...
Off-Campus Housing

Undergrads Living Off Campus
32%

Freshmen Living Off Campus
12%

Average Off-Campus Room & Board
$6,910

Average Rents
1 BR: $550
2 BR: $660
3 BR: $950

Best Time to Look for a Place
End of the academic year before the year you want to move off campus

Popular Areas
East Pointe area
North of campus in the

Compass Pointe
West of campus near the
fraternity houses

Students Speak Out On...
Off-Campus Housing

Q Apartment are easy to get
Fraternity houses offer members off-campus living after freshman year. Apartments are readily available. College Apartments and Compass Pointe are the best and most sought after places to live.

Q Apartments Are Easy to Find!
It's pretty easy to find a cheap apartment close to campus, but you have to be a senior to live off-campus.

Q Lots of Choices!
There are many different apartments to pick from with a variety of prices. You may have to sign up early to get one, but you can most likely find one that fits the needs you are trying to fulfill.

Q Good, and a Lot Cheaper Than on-Campus
There is decent availability, good availability for fraternities, and no availability for sororities. The main advantage is that it's so much cheaper than living on-campus because Valpo is so expensive.

Q Off Campus Housing
It is sometimes hard to find off campus housing-- the school doesn't really help. Also, housing off campus is usually in a "shadier" part of town, a.k.a. not the safest place. There are really nice apartments available through the university but the cost makes them unrealistic. Also, you only live off campus senior year.

💬 Off Campus Housing Isn't the Greatest
The off campus housing near the campus is fairly old. There are some new apartments on the North side of the campus, but other than those, most decent housing requires driving to school.

💬 Hard to Live Off Campus Prior to Senior Year.
Apartments and rentable houses can be found pretty close to campus, within the same range as Greek housing. I cant speak for the affordability of these housing options or how nice they are. Greek life is the best way to live off campus prior to Senior year.

💬 No Selection
Valparaiso only lets you live off campus if you are a senior. If you are a junior then you can live the university apartments which are ridiculously high. $1000/month per person.

The College Prowler Take On...
Off-Campus Housing

The University's rules on living off campus are that students have to reach senior status first. Only fraternity members can move off campus to their respective fraternity houses with junior status or below. However, if students are able to get enough credit hours to qualify for senior status before their actual senior year, they can move off campus early. Some students do not choose to leave their senior year because student dorms seem easier than finding a living space. However, apartments are relatively easy to find, and many landlords are fine with accomodating students for one year at a time.

The main issue is the proximity to campus. Most of the apartments are a good 15-minute walk from campus, so it is best if you have a car so you can commute. Uptown East Apartments is a good way to live on campus while having an apartment-style setting. It is across the street from campus, so it's very accessible to all of the buildings. Be aware that it is slightly more pricey, as it offers all amenities (big screen TV, desk, chair, bed, kitchen, etc.).

Prices for apartments and houses are not outrageous, but it is better to split the costs with multiple roommates. If living in an apartment off campus doesn't sound like your cup of tea, there are a few houses around town for rent. These are fun and might be worth the effort of living with friends and commuting to get to campus.

The College Prowler® Grade on Off-Campus Housing: B-

A high grade in Off-Campus Housing indicates that apartments are of high quality, close to campus, affordable, and easy to secure.

Diversity

The Lowdown On...
Diversity

African American
5%

Asian American
2%

Hispanic
4%

International
4%

Native American
1%

White
81%

Unknown
4%

Out-of-State Students
64%

Faculty Diversity
African American: 3%
Asian American: 3%
Hispanic: 1%
International: 2%
Native American: 0%
White: 88%
Unknown: 2%

Historically Black College/University?
No

Economic Status
Most students come from middle- to upper-middle-class families.

Gay Pride
Valpo has Alliance, a GLBT group, but the overall attitude on campus is not extremely tolerant of these lifestyles.

Most Common Religions
Christianity (largely Lutheran and Catholic) and Islam are the most prevalent religions.

Political Activity
College Republicans is the largest politically affiliated group on campus. College Democrats organize occasionally, and Valpo campus also has a College Libertarians group. There is also a group called PAL that meets to discuss hot topics in politics. They are not associated with any party.

Minority Clubs on Campus
The minority clubs on campus include LIVE (Latinos in Valparaiso for Excellence), BSO (Black Student Organization), and VISA (Valparaiso International Student Association).

Students Speak Out On...
Diversity

Q Meeting Someone New
I am orignally from Pittsburgh, so upon coming to Valparaiso I did not know anyone. After a few days of being on campus however, I met many people from all across the US. Most of the students are from Illinois, but they all have different ethnic backgrounds.

Q Diversity Is a Goal of Valpo.
Valpo has pushed diversity for a long time. There is a wide variety of students from different countries and religions. Valpo is very open to all different types of people.

Q A Lot of More Wealthy White Students, but Definitely Economic and Racial Diversity
Most of the students are white that have at least a middle level of income because tuition is high. But the university makes lots of scholarships available to everyone and of course admits people based on grades and not because of skin color.

Q Suburb
It's like living in the nearer suburbs, except with lots of international students

Q Getting There, but Still in Need of Improvement
Though there are a lot of international students on campus, it doesn't seem as if the local and international groups often mix. Unfortunately Valpo's campus is prominently white, and this is reflected in a lot of the cliques you see on campus.

Q Decent Diversity, but Not Much Racially Speaking

Valpo is like 85% white if I guessed off the top of my head. It's richness of diversity is in its foreign-exchange programs, political diversity. I don't care for politics and am American so these don't apply to me really, but it's there. There is little religious diversity as most of the school is Christian and Lutheran. A vast majority of the student population is middle to upper middle class white people.

Q Typical for a Small, Private School

There isn't a whole lot of diversity on campus, especially in the Greek community. Valpo is not terribly un-diverse, but it is mostly white. However, that is typical of a small, private, Lutheran college.

Q Open but homogenous

Valparaiso is pretty open to diversity, but it is a pretty homogenous student population.

The College Prowler Take On...
Diversity

If you are looking for diversity and the opportunity to meet and mix with students of different races and ethnicity, Valpo might not be the place for you. The minority population on campus is exactly that—the minority. There are some international students, but they tend to stick together and are further removed from campus. Many live in 807 Mound, which is a housing unit close to the fraternity houses. While there may not be much ethnic diversity on campus, the religious and political diversity is pretty average. Since we are a Lutheran campus, there are obviously a large number of Christians on campus, but there are quite a few students that believe in different religions like Islam.

The University continuously tries to make campus a more diverse place. Approximately 10 percent of the students are from foreign countries, so the numbers are much larger than they seem when you physically walk around campus. New international programs are getting started to help Valpo appeal to many different kinds of students. While there is not an overwhelmingly diverse student population, most students are accepting of all different sorts of beliefs, backgrounds, and status. There is little to no tension among various groups.

The College Prowler® Grade on
Diversity: C-

A high grade in Diversity indicates that ethnic minorities and international students have a notable presence on campus and that students of different economic backgrounds, religious beliefs, and sexual preferences are well-represented.

Guys & Girls

The Lowdown On...
Guys & Girls

Female Undergrads
53%

Male Undergrads
47%

Birth Control Available?

Yes: Only for medical reasons from the Health Center

Social Scene

Students at Valpo tend to be very outgoing and involved. Most students are members of multiple clubs or organizations. Valpo students are pretty supportive of on-campus activities; plays and concerts generally sell out, and the Union Board events (free movies, trips, guest entertainers) are always popular. Students also like to go to neighboring Merrillville to shop at the mall or go to the movies in one of the larger theaters. Most Valpo kids have traveled to Chicago at one time or another during their years at VU. Students tend to do these things in groups. They also attend fraternity events and parties in droves.

Hookups or Relationships?

Fraternity parties result in your average number of hookups, but many Valpo students seem to gravitate toward serious and long-term relationships. Some get married while still in school; many get married following graduation.

Dress Code

The dress code varies with the individual and the day of the week. There is no mandatory dress code. You might see someone in his or her Sunday best walking next to someone in their pajamas, and they'll both be headed to the same class. Whether you wear your pajamas everyday, dress up, or maintain something in between is completely up to you. You'll see punk or goth styles occasionally, but it's much more common to see Valpo students who look like they've just stepped out of a Gap commercial. Preppy.

Did You Know?

Top Places to Find Guys & Girls:

- Frat parties
- Intramural sports
- Residence halls

Top Places to Hook Up:

- Frat parties
- Local bars
- Off-campus parties
- Residence halls
- Campus activities and groups

Students Speak Out On...
Guys & Girls

Q Good, Everyone Is Friendly
I really like the people at Valpo. There's a general good quality to the student population. The small school atmosphere allows you to be friends with a good portion of the school, if you be social and go to parties and stuff.

Q Variety of People
At Valpo, there is a large amount of basic hard working college students, partiers, geeks, indies, and some rockers. A good amount of geeky, chill, and cool people. There's a moderate amount of foreign students. It's nice to have them but they live over at the international house. I wish that they would mingle the foreigners with the Americans more.

Q It's Pretty Average
I think Valpo has a great mix of every kind of person. Most people wear jeans and t-shirts, but it's not strange to see people dressed up or dressed down. I'd say we're a pretty average-looking campus, too.

Q Boys Usually Lacking for Relationships
Everyone is really friendly here, but overall the guys are a little lacking. There is definitely a range of personalities, but the good guys are usually already taken. It's a waiting game to see who breaks up when, but the good relationship guys are quickly snatched up.

Q Girls Girls Girls
almost every girl is just out for the looks, there are not that many good looking girls on campus, the ones that are not even that good looking think they are drop dead gorgous.

Alot of them have mommy and daddy pay for everything so alot of them are stuck up. And if you try holding the door open for one of them about 1/3 will say thank your or smile, the rest will just keep on walking or talking on their cell phone.

Q Valpo Vision
Most people are from the Midwest. There are some pretty girls. The guys aren't the hottest but usually are really great people-- no tools at this school.

Q Valpo in All Honesty
----------------------Looks-Men: AverageWomen: Poor----------------------------------Dress-Casual mostly. You won't find hipsters here. A few bro's and a few fashionable women. It's pretty lax in that regard.----------------------Social Life-It can be hard to find things to do on weekends. The frats will have parties, but if that stuff isn't for you your best bet is a movie or game with friends. You will learn to make your own fun. Keep in mind that this is a DRY CAMPUS, so if you are doing anything with booze you have to be careful at least. OR you could actually follow the rules set by the institution you decided to give all your money to.Additionally, this school can also be a little strange. I have been stopped from playing Poker by the RA's because gambling is not allowed and other pretty silly things like that.Members of the opposite sex cannot be in your dorm room after 2:00 a.m. typically. But again if you do have someone in your room later just be careful not to do something stupid and you should be fine.----------------------Relationships-Not going to lie, a lot of women are here to get their Mrs. degree...----------------------

Q Awful
All guys are jerks and think they are awesome because they're in frats.

The College Prowler Take On...
Guys & Girls

"Average" is the most commonly used word when asking anyone at Valpo about the physical attributes of the opposite sex. There are few good-looking ones wandering around, but there's no promising that they aren't taken. The good guys are usually taken; the good girls are usually taken. A lot of Valpo students end up finding the loves of their lives here. The variety of the students, however, is pretty strong. There is a good mix of jocks, geeks, creative artists, and average joes living on campus. Unfortunately, once you feel like you've exhausted all of the options on campus, you are pretty much done until college is over. It is much harder to meet people off campus and from other schools than if you click with someone that goes to Valpo as well, but it is possible.

The social scene is what you make of it. There are plenty of activities to get involved in, or you can just choose to stay in your room and watch movies with friends. There's a decent mix of people who choose to go out and who choose to stay in. There are always fraternity or house parties on the weekend, but Valpo is a dry campus, so be careful when coming back. Other than that, there are always things to do in Chicago for date nights and weekends.

Guys: B

The College Prowler® Grade on
Guys & Girls

A high grade for Guys or Girls indicates that the students on campus is attractive, smart, friendly, and engaging, and that the school has a decent gender ratio.

Girls: C

Athletics

The Lowdown On...
Athletics

Athletic Association
NAA
NCAA

Athletic Division
NCAA Division I-AA

Athletic Conferences
Football: Pioneer Football League
Basketball: Horizon League

School Colors
Brown and gold

School Nickname/ Mascot
Crusader

Men Playing Varsity Sports
273: 21%

Women Playing Varsity Sports
138: 10%

Men's Varsity Sports
Baseball
Basketball
Football
Soccer
Swimming and diving
Tennis
Track and field

Women's Varsity Sports
Basketball
Soccer
Softball
Swimming and diving
Tennis
Track and field
Volleyball

Intramurals
Badminton
Basketball
Billiards
Bowling
Cornhole
Dodgeball
Floor hockey
Foosball
Football
Golf
Kickball
Racquetball
Soccer
Softball
Swimming
Table tennis
Tennis
Ultimate Frisbee
Volleyball
Wallyball
Water basketball

Club Sports
Badminton
Fencing
Soccer (men's, women's)
Tennis
Ultimate Frisbee
Volleyball

Athletic Fields & Facilities
ARC Pool
Athletics Recreation Center (ARC)
Brown Field
The Course at Aberdeen
Eastgate Field
Emory G. Bauer Field
Fitness Center
Valpo Softball Field
Valpo Tennis Complex

Most Popular Sports
Basketball (men's and women's), volleyball

Most Overlooked Teams
Softball, men's soccer, swimming

School Spirit
Valpo's school spirit really shines when it comes to—you guessed it— basketball. The most blatant show of school spirit is the VUCRU—the student cheering section at the games. These students (most of the student body, in fact) dress to the nines in VU apparel and colors, sporting VU temporary tattoos, gold and brown face paint, and even gold wigs. VUCRU sponsors theme nights, so you'll often see these students with alien antennaes, coconut bras, or cowboy hats. They are loud, obnoxious, and do everything they can to harangue, irritate, and hassle the other team, its coaches, and the refs. Some of the most fun times at Valpo are had in the VUCRU! Tons of students even travel to see out-of-town VU games. One of the most notable instances of this was when students traveled hundreds of miles to watch VU play Duke during the 2003–2004 season. You'll also find school spirit running high during Homecoming and Spring Week when Union Board and Greek organizations put together campus competitions and sponsor campus-wide activities. Most students are proud to wear the brown and gold!

Getting Tickets
Tickets are usually not required for students. Your VU ID card will get you into the games free—even basketball games. Tickets are only required for off-campus sporting events or NCAA interleague games, where students get discounted rates. The only tickets that can be hard to get are extra tickets for men's basketball for friends and relatives. These are not expensive but can sell out for big games.

Best Place to Take a Walk

On campus—the sidewalks make a great place to run or ride. Off-campus trails include the trails at the Dunes and the Prairie Dogwood bicycle and walking trail.

Did You Know?

All of the athletics at Valpo are Division 1 besides football, which is Division 1 AA.

Valpo's basketball games are sometimes picked up by ESPN.

Students Speak Out On...
Athletics

Q A First Year
This year Valparaiso started a women's bowling team. With it only being their first year, they are already ranked 10th in the nation according to the NCAA. The girls are very hard-working and practice 3 days a week, working out everyday. The team has high hopes for next year and plan on attending the NCAA national championships.

Q VU BBALL
Basketball is really the only big sport here. Volleyball is pretty popular as well. Football is a complete joke; the whole team is still cocky even though they've lost 20+games in a row. The soccer teams are usually fairly good and their games can be fun to attend. Basketball games versus big schools like Purdue, ND, Kansas, MSU, and the all-too-famous Butler are exciting and fun.

Q Soccer Team Did Really Well
Soccer team did really well this year; other than that all other sports teams are pathetic.

Q Good for Both Cometitive Sports and IM
There is a wide variety of IM sports; leagues are fun for the most part. Campus does not have a huge interest in the school's varsity sports, but soccer for men and women and women's volleyball are our best.

Q Nothing Special
Valpo has a decent variety in sports, but little success in the mainstream ones. School spirit is rather poor too.

💬 Spirit Lacking. Talent Lacking

----------------------Student Involvement In Sports-Our basketball games are pretty well attended, but all of our sports are a joke and everyone knows it.----------------------Team Performance-Reliably terrible----------------------Fan Support-Well you will find people more supportive than I, but overall the support is little.----------------------School Spirit-Ask any student how our school song goes and I guarantee you they won't know it... unless they were a part of freshmen orientation where they lie to you about things such as School Spirit.----------------------Athletic Facilities-For non-sports people there is a new workout facility that is completely free AND it isn't half bad (not great though). +0.52 for Valpo. For athletes I have no idea what you get. It's better than what I get. That's all I know.----------------------Don't come here for the athletics, and I don't just mean for people in the stands. Potential athletes beware. We really aren't a good place for you to be if you want to go somewhere with your sport.

💬 Coaches aren't good

The football coaches should be fired. That's why we are terrible.

💬 Team Performance Football

Our football team is absolutely terrible and has been for some time. We're getting a new coach so hopefully it gets better.

The College Prowler Take On...
Athletics

For students, lately there have only been two sports worth attending: volleyball and basketball. Each year the attendance varies, but these two teams can draw in a large community and student crowd. The student section in the ARC is usually filled with the Pep Band and fans sporting brown and gold. There are many other athletic teams on campus, but they draw much smaller crowds.

There is a football team, but while decent, they have enormous trouble filling the stands for every home game, except Homecoming. The softball team is continuing to improve with each consecutive year's success, and in turn, is gaining more of a regular crowd. Most of the other Division I sports don't draw much of a crowd at all.

Many students also like to play sports. Intramurals are available to anyone who wants to play, and they are a great way for a large number of students to stay in shape and take a much needed break from studying. About half of the student body gets involved in at least one intramural sport. Many teams are created by Greek organizations, other clubs, residents sharing a wing, and groups of friends. The highly coveted champion t-shirt is the reward for winning tournaments.

The College Prowler® Grade on
Athletics: C+

A high grade in Athletics indicates that students have school spirit, that sports programs are respected, that games are well-attended, and that intramurals are a prominent part of student life.

Nightlife

The Lowdown On...
Nightlife

Cheapest Place to Get a Drink
Pepe's on Tuesdays

Primary Areas with Nightlife
Downtown Valpo
In town

Closing Time
3 a.m.

Useful Resources for Nightlife
www.metromix.com

Bar Listings

Bin Willy's
3530 Calumet Ave.
(219) 477-6778
Bin Willy's serves food, as well as being a local student bar. They host a DJ, as well as live bands on the weekends, and offer great specials.

Duffy's Place
1154 Axe Ave.
(219) 462-1057
Duffy's is not the first choice for students on a regular basis, but it has a large beer garden area open in the spring that is often used for Senior Week activities or welcome-back bashes.

Northside Tap Bar & Grill
712 Calumet Ave.
(219) 465-0885
www.northsidetap.com
Northside is often referred to as the 'townie bar,' meaning that most of its patrons tend to be locals, but many VU students head to Northside because it has great prices. You must be 21 to get in, and the carding policy is pretty strict. Northside also has live music from time to time, and they do serve good bar food and appetizers. There is no cover and parking is free.

Pastimes
175 Lincolnway
(219) 462-3786
Probably the best bar food for miles! Pastimes is more like your average Irish pub than a bar. This is the choice for students who want to go out and drink with friends but also have some quality food and conversation. It's quieter and more sophisticated than the other places.

Other Places to Check Out
Buddy and Pal's
El Salto
Martini's
Pepe's

Local Specialties
Goose Island
Old Style

Favorite Drinking Games
Beirut/Beer Pong
Flip Cup
Quarters

What to Do if You're Not 21
Cinemark
700 Porter Vale's Rd
Valparaiso
800-326-3264
There's always a movie on, and it's a popular place to go for those who don't want to partake in drinking festivities.

Frat parties
Mound or nearby
Valparaiso
Best thing to do when you're under 21 is to go to the frats.

Organization Parties
Many campus groups throw the occasional party, but campus rules about alcohol make this tricky. VISA holds dance parties on a regular basis, but as far as off-campus parties are concerned, you'd most likely have to hit up the frats.

Students Speak Out On...
Nightlife

Q Never Alone
The best perk about Valparaiso University if the the service the campus police provide. Every evening from the hours of 7 pm to 2 am the police operate a bus that can take students around campus. For safety purposes I think this is a great idea, no student ever has to walk alone around campus to get where they are going.

Q Nightlife
There is so much to do in Valpo! It's really close to Chicago, a big-time party-city. There are clubs for all ages and sure to be a party every night.

Q Good, but Discrete
Nightlife consists of a few bars, but mostly fraternity parties. Nothing exciting happens on-campus in regards to parties. Fraternity parties are easily accessed enough and plentiful, but discrete to counteract strict VUPD.

Q Pretty Good
Nightlife mostly involves going to frat parties. There are sometimes drinking in the dorms as well. Once you reach 21, people go out to the bars.

Q AVERAGE
If you want a nightlife you can find a nightlife. Enough said.

Q Nightlife Confined to Campus
There is always something to do, but it's on campus most of the times. Unless you go out into Chicago, you'll be on campus. Union Board puts on some activities that students

go to; otherwise you find a frat house to hang out at. There's always the good old fashioned watch a movie with friends route too.

It Would Be Better If It Wasn't a Dry Campus

There are fun things, but you can only go to so many dance parties before you get tired of them. They are so packed and hot that its hard to have a good time. If it were not a dry campus and those of us who were old enough could go out to drink it would be a lot more fun.

Not Much to Do

There really isn't much nightlife in Valpo. There's the hookah lounge and a few bars, but that's it.

The College Prowler Take On...
Nightlife

Nightlife at Valpo mostly revolves around the house parties and frat parties that are held throughout the week. A limited number of students go to the bars on a regular basis, but once you reach that golden age of 21, you will go... at least once. There are not a lot of options for bars around Valpo, but they are frequently visited by some Valpo students. They are sometimes smokey and crowded, so most people drink at home or at house parties.

Frat parties, on the other hand, are held often for students at campus. The most popular are the non-alcoholic dance parties that many students attend. There's a small cover charge that goes towards a philanthropy. Otherwise, there are the typical small gatherings at frats or off-campus houses that entertain many Valpo students. Most of the frat parties are overrun with freshmen and Greeks. Few non-Greek or non-freshmen take the time to head to the frat houses for a party.

The College Prowler® Grade on
Nightlife: B

A high grade in Nightlife indicates that there are many bars and clubs in the area that are easily accessible and affordable. Other determining factors include the number of options for the under-21 crowd and the prevalence of house parties.

Greek Life

The Lowdown On...
Greek Life

Freshman Men in Fraternities
26%

Freshman Women in Sororities
24%

Undergrad Men in Fraternities
24%

Undergrad Women in Sororities
20%

Number of Fraternities
9

Number of Sororities
7

Fraternities
Lambda Chi Alpha
Phi Kappa Psi
Phi Mu Alpha
Phi Sigma Kappa
Sigma Chi
Sigma Phi Epsilon
Sigma Pi
Sigma Tau Gamma
Theta Chi

Sororities
Chi Omega
Delta Delta Delta
Delta Xi Phi
Gamma Phi Beta
Kappa Delta
Kappa Kappa Gamma
Pi Beta Phi

Multicultural Colonies
Delta Xi Phi

Other Greek Organizations
Greek Judicial Board
Intrafraternity Council
Order of Omega
Panhellenic Council

Did You Know?

Greeks on campus host some of the most interesting events. Sigma Chi fraternity holds Derby Days—a week-long competition between all-female teams that serves as a fundraiser for charity—in the fall. The weekend after Easter, the fraternities and sororities hold Songfest in the Chapel of the Resurrection, which is a song-and-dance revue competition between the chapters. Phi Mu Alpha Sinfonia (the men's music fraternity) serenades female students by singing outside the dorms.

Students Speak Out On...
Greek Life

Q Greek Life
I feel that Greek life sculpts our social atmosphere. Especially as freshman, students don't know what to do exactly on the weekends and often there will be an event put on by the sororities or fraternities for them to attend.

Q To Be Greek or Not to Be
Here at Valpo its not a big deal if you do not become Greek. Even though I am Greek, I have many friends who aren't and they still are able to have fun on campus and feel like they are apart of the social scene on campus. There is also no pressure from Greek students to become Greek. Everyone makes their own decision about become Greek.

Q Go Greek
For such a small school, Greek life is pretty big. It's where all the parties are and where 34% of the students are. They throw fun parties and good events on campus. They are a great activity to use while at school here.

Q Greek Life Positive Image on Campus
There is no pressure to become Greek, but about 30-35% of our students do go Greek. All of the organizations are really involved in philanthropy and service projects. They overall have a positive image on campus.

Q Excellent for a Small School
Greek Life is excellent at Valpo for both fraternities and sororities. There is little in the way of hazing and none of the chapters are overly large like at state schools.

Approximately a third of the undergraduates are Greek. Housing is available fr fraternities, but not sororities. Sororities have a sorority dorm (Scheele).

Q Almost 20 % of Campus Is Involved in Greek Life

Greek life is a big part of our campus. Many social events revolve around Greek life.

Q Definitely a Small School

Granted, Greek life is very big here, yet the campus takes drinking way too seriously. The once-so-great frat row has turned into two frats; one being filled with weird guys, the other one being too selective. Drinking has to be hidden and kept secret or else you get arrested. But, there is no pressure to be Greek, and non-Greeks get along great with other Greeks. And Greeks here are actually cool and have personalities.

Q There Is Room for Improvement in Valpo Greek Life

Valpo is the smallest school to have its own police force for an university. For this, it is dangerous for fraternities and sororities to maximize the potential of socializing on weekends. The precautions required for risk management are a headache that shouldn't be there. Sororities are not allowed to possess houses at Valpo; that's discrimination.

The College Prowler Take On...
Greek Life

Greeks are a large part of the inner workings of campus, The numbers indicate that a little over 30 percent of the campus is involved in a Greek organization, but often it can feel like 70 percent, While it is definitely possible to live a full and happy life on campus without being Greek, people involved in Greek life will say that pledging is the best way to make friends and get involved on campus, Valpo has a deferred recruitment, so freshmen are able to get accustomed to campus before deciding whether or not to go through recruitment,

People involved in Greek life also typically get involved with many other organizations on campus such as Student Government and Union Board, This tends to make it seem like Greeks are everywhere, but there are plenty of organizations to get involved in that do not involve the Greeks,

However, if you do decide to go Greek, you would get inolved automatically in many philanthropy and service events, Each sorority and fraternity has a charity that they fundraise for at some point in the year, They try to get all students to participate in their fundraiser through some fun activity like Phi Psi 500, Derby Days, and Kappa Kasino, People also get involved in a variety of service projects, like helping at Café Manna or doing Day of Caring, Either way, Greek life is usually carries a positive image around campus, but there is no pressure to join,

The main downside to Greek life is that sororities on campus live in Scheele Hall in separate wings... For the rest of this editorial, visit collegeprowler.com.

The College Prowler® Grade on Greek Life: B+

A high grade in Greek Life indicates that sororities and fraternities are not only present, but also active on campus. Other determining factors include the variety of houses available and the respect the Greek community receives from the rest of the campus.

Drug Scene

The Lowdown On...
Drug Scene

Most Popular Drugs
Alcohol
Marijuana

Alcohol-Related Referrals
96

Alcohol-Related Arrests
9

Drug-Related Referrals
0

Drug-Related Arrests
9

Drug Counseling Programs
Student Counseling and Development Center
LaPorte Avenue
(219) 464-5002
Personal counseling services; Drug and alcohol abuse prevention presentations and programs; the SUDDS program for students who have minor issues with alcohol; CARE classes are available for students with a more intense alcohol addiction.

Students Speak Out On...
Drug Scene

Q Present Enough to Be Fun
I haven't seen much drug use on campus, but know several people that smoke weed off campus. I have never seen any hard drugs being used, and know of only one person to have cocaine access. Alcohol is plentiful, and many people drink in the dorms, but it's so hard and discrete because of Valpo's enforced dry campus. Most of the drinking is at fraternity parties, and over a third of the undergraduates are Greek. Overall, I feel that Valpo has a healthy and safe drug and alcohol presence, but naturally that will vary with the kind of parties you go to. Some fraternities are typically deemed unsafe whereas other fraternities are reputed for being safe and responsible. Sororities don't have houses at Valpo and don't apply.

Q Drinking Accepted, Drugs Must Be Hidden
Drinking is pretty widely accepted even though it is a dry campus. It is visible and anyone can access it. Drugs are very much frowned upon as a whole and is very subtle when it takes place

Q It Is Here
I would say that drugs other then alcohol are hard to come by. A student would have to actively seek them out. alcohol is available and much easier to come by.

Q Not a Whole Lot
While the campus is supposed to be tobacco free and a dry campus, there are a fair amount of smokers. It is easy to avoid alcohol if you choose to be around those kinds of people

Q Not Crazy

There is definitely alcohol on the campus as well as in the frat houses, but it's pretty well hidden to the outside. The frats are very cautious about making sure everyone is inside and in a safe place. Policy enforcement has gotten better over the years (so I've heard) THey can and will arrest but you usually have to be pretty messed up to get pulled over. Drugs aren't a big thing - marijuana is the most common, but I feel that will be everywhere.

Q Dry Campus?

I know drinking goes on a lot even though we are a dry campus. However, I feel as though it's mainly not visible; you really only have to get involved if you want.

Q Drugs easy enough to obtain

There is a fair amount of drug use but you won't see it unless you're going out to look for the drugs or alcohol. If you're looking, they're easy enough to obtain. Valpo is uptight, so it's easy to get caught. Most people drink more than anything.

Q You Can Get Em

Drugs..yeah you can get em

The College Prowler Take On...
Drug Scene

Finding drugs on campus is a difficult task. The portion of the campus population that participates in drug use is minimal. Just about every student knows more people in his/her high school class who did drugs than people around campus who do drugs. The most used drug, not including alcohol, would be marijuana, but it is used by a limited amount of students so it is not noticeable.

At Valpo, there are the people who have tried this or done that, but if you have to choose a "drug" that gets the most use on campus, it would be alcohol. However, if you don't drink there is no pressure to do so. Even at the bigger fraternity parties, no one forces anyone to drink. It is really easy for drinkers and non-drinkers to coexist with each other, which makes the atmosphere on campus really positive.

The College Prowler® Grade on Drug Scene: C

A high grade in the Drug Scene indicates that drugs are not a noticeable part of campus life; drug use is not visible, and no pressure to use them seems to exist.

Campus Strictness

The Lowdown On...
Campus Strictness

Students Are Most Likely to Get Caught...
Being too noisy in the dorms
Downloading music
Having a member of the opposite sex in a room after visitation hours
Parking illegally
Propping open the side doors to the residence halls
Underage drinking and/or public intoxication
Violating the Honor Code (Valpo's academic honesty policy)

Visitation Policies
You can have guests of the opposite sex in your room until 1 a.m. on weeknights and 2 a.m. on weekends. Your floor can vote to make the lounge available to both genders at all times of day.

Did You Know?

VUPD is not a security force but an actual police department. Officers are trained the same as other city police officers.

Students Speak Out On...
Campus Strictness

Q Really Strict
This school is strict about all of its policies. That cant be stressed enough.

Q Strictness
I believe that the strictness of the university has a lot to do on where you live. I am talking about the RA's in particular. I live in Brandt Hall and both of the RA's on my floor are awesome. They aren't super picky on all the rules but if something is getting out of hand they will step in and usually all it takes is them to say something and that the end of it. I have never heard of anyone on our floor getting wrote up for anything. I think if you show the RA's respect they will respect you back.

Q Very good and fair
I think being strict can be more beneficial for the university. If it's a risk you are willing to take then you should be willing to accept the consequences.

Q Strict Overall. It's Not a State School.
Valpo is a private school and a dry campus. The party scene is very alive and well, but very contained and small. VUPD will stop people regularly. I've been to multiple state schools where students didn't make a second thought on carrying open alcohol containers in the streets, driving drunk, and sometimes even passing out shots in the football parking lot before the homecoming game. Not a chance in hell can you get away with that at Valpo. The dorms have fairly strict rules, but it mostly depends on your

RA. I was never upset be Valpo's rules or policies outside of making my fraternity's risk managing a very serious concern lest we be arrested by campus police.

💬 Seems average

From what I've heard, if the police catch you drinking, you go to jail. But tons of people drink all the time and don't get caught. Other than that, it mostly depends on how strict your RA is.

💬 VUPD should relax

VUPD needs to chill out. They are way too strict-didn't they go to college too?

💬 Alcohol not hard to get into dorms

While the college doesn't allow alcohol in dorms officially, it's really not that hard to get it in and have some.

💬 TOO STRICT

If they were a little less strict, things wouldn't get so out of control.

The College Prowler Take On...
Campus Strictness

How strict the campus seems depends on whether you are looking at VUPD or Judicial Board policies and punishments (out of dorm vs. in dorm). VUPD handles drug and alcohol issues both in and out of the dorms, but the RAs and the dorm J-Boards handle other serious and non-serious write-ups. Each J-Board is a group of students elected by the dorm to hand out punishments for noise violations, alcohol use, curfew violations, and door propping. The J-Board punishments are notoriously more lenient than those handed out by VUPD.

Punishments from J-Board could be simply writing an essay on why what you did is wrong and why the rule is necessary. More serious crimes are handled by the VUPD. Many students will complain about the policies if caught drinking. If the police catch you, they will take you to jail where you sit for six hours before bail can be posted. There used to be a saying that "you haven't experienced Valpo until you've been arrested." Your record can be expunged with some community service and classes, though.

Overall, people complain about the police often, but they do increase the safety around campus. Most people feel that the police affect campus in a positive way as long as you learn to respect the rules, or at least be prepared to accept the consequences.

The College Prowler® Grade on
Campus Strictness: C

A high Campus Strictness grade implies an overall lenient atmosphere; police and RAs are fairly tolerant, and the administration's rules are flexible.

Parking

The Lowdown On...
Parking

Parking Services
Valparaiso University Police Department
816 Union St.
(219) 464-5430
www.valpo.edu/vupd

Approximate Parking Permit Cost
$60 per semester

Student Parking Lot
Yes: There are 27 student lots (mostly for commuters) spread around campus).

Freshmen Allowed to Park
Yes

Common Parking Tickets

Driving or parking on grass: $25
Fire lane: $50
Handicapped zone: $50
No parking zone: $50

Getting a Parking Permit

Freshmen may obtain permits if they live 500 or more miles from Valpo, or if they have an off-campus job. Resident permits (sophomores and juniors) are available to any and all upperclassmen. Senior parking permits are available only to those students with senior class standing, and allow those students to park in resident or commuter parking areas. Commuter permits are available to any and all enrolled students who live off campus, including fraternity members.

Did You Know?

Best Places to Find a Parking Spot:

• Large lot across from the Union
• Anywhere between 5 p.m. and 2 a.m.
• LaPorte Avenue

Good Luck Getting a Parking Spot Here!

• Guild/Memorial lot during a basketball game
• Outside Brandt and Wehrenberg halls
• Directly outside Scheele is also difficult since it is so near the Freshman Residential Halls, and the school did not allocate a large amount of parking spaces there.

Students Speak Out On...
Parking

Q Parking Is Ok, but Could Be Better
There are a couple of places to park on campus, but they aren't really that close together so if one is full it takes some time to get to the next one. Unless you're going off campus or are a commuter, its just as easy to walk. Things aren't that far apart.

Q Freshmen Can't Drive
Unless you live over 500 miles away or have an off-campus job, freshmen can't drive, but there isn't much need for a car on our campus. You can walk to Wal-mart or Target if needed, and you can always take the V-line, which is a bus service into town. There is a parking garage on campus, and I believe a permit costs $100 a year.

Q Availability good
There is usually available parking most places.

Q Cars Are Nice, but Not Necessary
First of all, freshman are not allowed to have cars unless they live more than 500 miles away. Everything is fairly close to campus and I survived my freshman year without a car. Now, they have a city bus that will take students to Walmart and Target for shopping. A parking permit costs $100 which I thought was high until I found out some of my friends at other schools pay $300-600. There is a good number of parking spaces on campus, but it is only close to the dorms. It is hard to park close to the Union or the Athletic Recreation Center. However, everything on campus is walkable so there is no need for a car.

Difficult to Describe

There is some parking, but it's easier to just walk to class. And the parking pass for parking in designated areas of campus are damn expensive.

Average Parking

For the number of students at Valpo, there are a good number of parking spots. However, parking passes are expensive and Freshman typically are not allowed cars on campus. There is one parking garage.

Valpo Is a "Walking" Campus

Valpo has tried to become a more pedestrian friendly campus as of late. That, in turn, makes having a vehicle somewhat difficult. Parking around buildings for classes is limited. Most parking is a little bit of a walk from classes. Parking lots are typically taken over during sporting events by fans. There is only one parking garage, but there are plans for more in the future.

Parking Sucks

The commuter lot by the engeneering and meteorology building always has someone hawking around trying to get a spot and parking tickets are not really given out to much, the lazy people go and park there when they dont have a pass and never get caught.

The College Prowler Take On...
Parking

Parking, at times, causes a lot of stress and frustration, especially when students are searching for a spot close to a residence hall or a class that they are late for. The lots are not necessarily right next to any buildings because they are placed on the edges of campus. The University is attempting to make Valpo primarily a walking campus, and that is ultimately the best way to get around. No matter where you park, you are going to have to walk to get anywhere, so unless you are a commuter, a car is not beneficial for getting around campus.

VUPD is in charge of issuing parking passes and ticketing, but officers have admitted that VUPD does not limit the number of passes based on the number of parking spaces available to students. Thus, during the busiest times of the day, it will take a while to find an open parking spot, especially one near the desired destination.

The College Prowler® Grade on
Parking: B

A high grade in the Parking section indicates that parking is both available and affordable, and that parking enforcement isn't overly severe.

Transportation

The Lowdown On...
Transportation

Best Ways to Get Around Town
Walk
Bike
Catch a ride with a friend (or bribe an upperclassman)
Drive your car

Public Transit
ChicaGo Dash
(877) 7GO-DASH
www.chicagodash.com
Express service between Valparaiso and Chicago

Coach USA Tri-State
www.coachusa.com/tristateunitedlimo
Shuttle to the Midway and O'Hare airports

V-Line
(219) 476-9393
www.valpo.us/v-line
Valparaiso City Transit System

Safety Escort Services
Valpo Escort Van
(219) 464-6040
Daily 6 p.m.–2 a.m.

Best Ways to Get to the Airport

CoachUSA/Tri-State Coach Lines, from Merrillville to O'Hare or Midway (219) 944-1200 or (800) 248-8747 Ride to South Shore Line which goes into Millennium Station in Chicago.

Take a cab or get a ride to the Gary Airport. A cab ride to the airport costs around $85 (Midway), $95 (O' Hare), or $40 (Gary).

The bus stops in the K-Mart parking lot on US 30 in Merrillville.

Nearest Airport

Gary-Chicago Airport
6001 Industrial Highway
(219) 949-9722
www.garychicagoairport.com
Located about 22 miles from campus.

Midway International Airport
5700 S. Cicero Ave.
(773) 582-8239
flychicago.com/about/Midway

O'Hare International Airport
10000 W. O'Hare
(312) 953-1422
flychicago.com/about/OHare

Nearest Passenger Bus

Greyhound
1000 W. Fourth Ave., Gary
(800) 229-9424 or (219) 886-3041
www.greyhound.com
There is not a Valparaiso bus terminal for Greyhound, but there is one in Gary, Ind.

Nearest Passenger Train

Amtrak Union Station
225 S. Canal St., Chicago
(800) USA-RAIL
www.amtrak.com
Valparaiso does not have an Amtrak station. Take the NICTD commuter train (the South Shore Line) into Chicago and use the Chicago Amtrak station.

Students Speak Out On...
Transportation

Q Pretty Good
The V line can take you to WalMart and to the Chesterton train station. And the Late Van service is great for lazy people.

Q Options, Not Totally Utilized
The university offers free in-campus transportation, as well as free town transportation to get around. Not many students use it though

Q Walking Is Best!
There is good public transportation for the university. There is bad parking, so walking is encouraged. I do not have a car, and I do not have problems with transportation.

Q Access to Public Transportation, but Too Little Parking
I do not have a car on campus, but I have noticed that there are too few parking spots on campus for the number of student who have cars. For people without cars who want to get around, the V-Line is very convenient.

Q Fairly Good
There is a V-line bus that picks students up on campus regularly and takes them to local places, or the train station. There's also a bus that will take you to Chicago called the Chicago Dash. If you want to go farther away though, you'll probably need a car.

Q Transportation Not an Issue

----------------------Convenience-There is always a bus going around that you can call for a ride, and it is still free.----------------------Cost-The most popular mode of transportation is personal car which many students have. If you do not have one personally, just make friends with someone who does. Not a big deal. The cost will be for your own gas.----------------------Need for Campus-Little need for transportation because we are not a big campus.----------------------Local-They have buses that will go to the nearby Target and other destinations if you need to do shopping. This comes in handy during the winter months.---------------------Long Distance-On weekends they have a bus that goes to Chicago which is pretty cool, but I don't know how much it costs. I would assume that it is reasonable for college students. Other than that you have train options both Metra and Amtrak. I have used these trains to go to both Chicago as well as MSU, and it's fantastic.----------------------

Q Above Average Transportation

Between 6:00 pm and 2:00 am, there are transportation vans that students can call to go from point A to point B. There is also a transportation service called the V-Line that runs set routes around town and to the train station. The train station is 20 minutes north of the city.

Q Not Much Transportation Available

Valpo is a small town and a small school so transportation isn't too important - you can walk most places. There is a city bus that runs during the week to Target and Wal-Mart among other places. At night, there is a van for going about campus in the dark if you feel unsafe.

The College Prowler Take On...
Transportation

There is not much public transportation in Valpo, but campus transportation is much easier anyways. The V-Line will pick up students around campus and bring them to set spots around the city free of charge. The destinations include Wal-Mart, Target, the movie theater, the train station, and downtown. The Student Escort Service drives around and picks students up at any spot around campus, even the frat houses. One van goes off campus into the surrounding areas where many apartments are located. If you want a ride from one building to another, and want to make sure the van actually stops for you to get in, just dial L.A.I.D. on your phone. It runs from 6 p.m. to 2 a.m. and will take you anywhere within a 2-mile radius of campus.

Campus is small enough that during the day, transportation systems like buses available at state schools aren't needed. You can easily walk from one end of campus to the other in 15–20 minutes. Downtown Valparaiso is accessible by walking 20 minutes, and once you're downtown, everything is spread across three or four blocks. Only if you need to get to the north end of town or to neighboring Merrillville does a ride or a car becomes necessary. Freshmen are not typically allowed cars, so make friends with an upperclassman if you ever need a ride. If you break your leg or something of the sort, the Valparaiso University Police Department can take you to class if necessary.

The College Prowler® Grade on Transportation: B

A high grade for Transportation indicates that campus buses, public buses, cabs, and rental cars are readily-available and affordable. Other determining factors include proximity to an airport and the necessity of transportation.

Weather

The Lowdown On...
Weather

Temperature Averages
Spring – High: 60 °F
Spring – Low: 39 °F
Summer – High: 82 °F
Summer – Low: 61 °F
Fall – High: 62 °F
Fall – Low: 43 °F
Winter – High: 34 °F
Winter – Low: 19 °F

What to Pack
Rain boots

Precipitation Averages
Spring: 3.47 in.
Summer: 4.13 in.
Fall: 3.48 in.
Winter: 2.27 in.

Students Speak Out On...
Weather

💬 I Love the Weather
We have all the different types of weather. You know this when coming to Valpo. Deal with it

💬 Winter brings lots of snow
It is wonderful to have the four seasons in Valpo. We come in the fall with some really hot weather, which is great for the Dunes. Then, there is plenty of snow in the winter for great iceskating and sledding or staying in and watching movies. The spring is rainy, but it is always wonderful to see green again!

💬 Annoying, but Expected
We live in the midwest. People knew that coming here. It should not be unexpected that we have to deal with snow.

💬 Used to it
I was born and raised in the Valpo area, so I am used to the weather that we have. It doesnt affect my campus experience at all.

💬 Its Pretty Ok.
A lot of people complain about the weather here. I really like snow and rain though, so I don't mind it. And campus is just great in the spring when the sun is shining and the flowers are blooming.

💬 They Don't Call It Valpo-Rain-Snow for Nothing
It precipitates a lot, but classes are rarely cancelled and the walk can be long and treacherous. But yeah, when it's nice everyone is outside.

💬 Four Seasons

Four distinct seasons, but winter can be long sometimes. If you like snow and hoodie weather, you'll love Valpo.

💬 It's Very Windy.

I'm not a fan of the cold but the wind is worse. However, campus is really pretty and when it's nice out (which is only for about 4 out of the 12 months) I LOVE being outside. Winter can be ok too I guess. Snow is pretty. It just lasts FOREVER.

The College Prowler Take On...
Weather

The most common thing students complain about on campus is the weather. The mild fall and spring seasons are often forgotten as soon as winter kicks in. Because Valpo is only about twenty miles from Lake Michigan, most people blame the sometimes unpredictable weather on the lake effect. There are years where it is still in the fifties in December, but after break it is consistently freezing.

Snow piles up quickly in the winter months, but the plows on campus work pretty well to make all the classes accessible, so do not expect them to cancel. All the snow that the Midwest gets is manageable, but the worst part about the weather is most arguably the wind. In comparison to Valparaiso, Chicago does not seem like the windy city. Here there are perfect pathways that make the blistering cold wind blow straight into your face on the way to class and on the way back.

No matter how bad the weather gets, students get used to it. Classes do not get cancelled unless the professor cannot get on campus, which sometimes makes it difficult for commuter students. Just make sure you pack a scarf, gloves, and a warm winter jacket. Most often jeans and a sweatershirt are all that is needed. Valpo rains an insane amount and usually it lasts all day, so rainboots are the most necessary footwear to bring. Umbrellas always break because of the wind, so you may need to invest in a raincoat as well. Also, be prepared for the warm weeks in the beginning and end of the year by bringing a swimsuit and flip flops to go to the beach (it's only twenty minutes away!).

The College Prowler® Grade on

A high Weather grade designates that temperatures are mild and rarely reach extremes, that the campus tends to be sunny rather than rainy, and that weather is fairly consistent rather than unpredictable.

VALPARAISO UNIVERSITY

Report Card Summary

B- ACADEMICS	**B** GUYS
C LOCAL ATMOSPHERE	**C** GIRLS
B HEALTH & SAFETY	**C+** ATHLETICS
B- COMPUTERS	**B** NIGHTLIFE
B- FACILITIES	**B+** GREEK LIFE
B- CAMPUS DINING	**C** DRUG SCENE
B- OFF-CAMPUS DINING	**C-** CAMPUS STRICTNESS
B- CAMPUS HOUSING	**B** PARKING
B- OFF-CAMPUS HOUSING	**B** TRANSPORTATION
C- DIVERSITY	**C** WEATHER

Overall Experience

Students Speak Out On...
Overall Experience

Q **Great. Best Decision of My Life.**
I am studying meteorology, and Valpo is among the very top in the nation for undergraduate meteorology. Valpo is very expensive, but I get my money's worth because of the meteorology program. I'm a C student mostly at Valpo for Met, but would probably be an A student if I went to a lesser school. We have senior and junior courses that are typically seen in graduate programs, very competent and intelligent professors, and a small family-like major. The people are what make Valpo. It's a small school where everyone practically knows each other. I am a Sigma Pi and am happy to say that my brothers are the reason why I love to come back to Valpo every year. Greek life is excellent for a school so small, and there is little to no hazing unlike at large state schools. The small size of Valpo is one of its

greatest advantages for all students. Professors are more like friends and the departments are so small that you get to know all of your fellow students. I love Valpo and recommend it to all.

Q Valparaiso University Is a Great School!

Between the variety of majors, clubs, religious life, and academic opportunities, Valpo is great. Even though it is small, it has big opportunities. The academic programs at Valpo are generally highly regarded, and many Valpo grads go on to be very successful in life. Although it is affiliated with Lutheranism, you do not have to be Lutheran or Christian at all to enjoy your experience at Valpo. The diversity of people is also great as Valpo attracts students from all over the world.

Q Go VU!

I am so glad I came to Valpo. I have found some of the best friends in the world, and the professors really care about students. If you are committed to working (and playing) hard, it will totally pay off in the end.

Q Friendly People

My professors are typically very nice, helpful, and smart. Almost everyone who works at Valpo is kind and helpful. The only exceptions is the sometimes ridiculously harsh enforcement drinking (not even underage drinking but of people who are 21 as well) by the VUPD. I'm also having trouble with RA's and an RLC who do not respect their residents. However, the excellence of the professors outweighs these negatives. Additionally, the Valpo community is supportive and friendly.

Q Work Hard, Play Moderately

At this school you definitely have to work hard; it is hard academically for Pre med and nursing and engineering. To what may be considered joke classes such as comm and PR, it is still tough academically. Parties are able to be found on Thurs-Sat, but if you don't want to find them you won't. If you do they're there. But there is no pressure to party ALL the time. And it's just fun.

Experience

My experience here at Valpo has been awesome! All the guys on the soccer team are my best friends and I always have a great time with them. It also seems that everyone else on campus is pretty nice for the most part too. I have made a lot of new friends in all my classes to and the classes all seem to be fun most of the time. The only down side for me is my roommate who basically just sits around and plays video games all day. It doesn't effect me too much besides making our room smell bad quite often. Besides that I love it here and would definitely come here if I had to decide all over again.

Go Here for the People.

The people are what make Valparaiso a good school. It's a dry campus, and that can be a big inconvenience and lead to some trouble for the party seeking crowd, but if you look and aren't dumb about it you can steer clear of any trouble. The university is a 'walking campus' so you're supposed to walk everywhere, but that's made difficult by paths that lead to nowhere and take you in roundabout ways to get to where you want to go. I highly recommend Greek life on campus, it allows you to meet a lot of new people and get involved with things on campus. Required classes such as 'CORE' and 'Theo 200' are a severe pain, but once you get into the classes that suit you, the teachers are knowledgeable and nice and will accommodate to your needs (for the most part).

Not the Greatest, but...

Something most people don't realize until they actually start here is that the majority of students don't love this place. I didn't love it here in the beginning but it has grown on me a bit. The people are good though, they're what make it worthwhile. There are a lot of service opportunities on campus which I enjoy. Plenty of alternative spring break options is one of its strengths. I'll be ready to leave this place when the time comes.

The College Prowler Take On...
Overall Experience

When trying to determine the best part about their VU experience, most students recount the great friends and the encouraging atmosphere the professors work hard to create. A great advantage to the students at Valpo is the willingness of professors to speak with you, even if you aren't in their class or even their department. If a change of majors might sound good, any professor from any department is willing to take time out of his/her schedule and talk about the department and its programs. The education and chances to learn from professors, who are there to teach first and research/publish second, is by far the best aspect of Valpo. It feels like a lot of work at the beginning because the classes are designed to make thought and discussion happen on a daily basis, but the work definitely pays off at graduation when you realize how much you've learned.

Students consistently comment that they have left Valpo with lasting friendships and a deep appreciation for learning. Valpo is a one-of-a-kind place that just seems to draw you in. The community aspect is the most commented on portion of life at Valpo because it is so strong. Campus truly becomes your home.

A negative part of the college experience is the strictness coming from VUPD, but most students feel that the positives highly outweigh the feelings of being treated like a child at times. Most students would choose Valpo again if they had to start over. If you are looking for a strong community and caring professors, Valpo really should be on your list.

The Inside Scoop

The Lowdown On...
The Inside Scoop

School Slang
'Berg: Wehrenberg Hall (either the cafeteria or the dorm itself)
Ark: ARC (Athletics Recreation Center)
CC: Christ College, Mueller Hall (the honors college—both the college and the building)
Chapel: The Chapel of the Resurrection
Chapel Meadow: The grassy area behind the Chapel
DA: Desk Attendant
The Dungeon: The basement of Mueller Hall
Fish Tank Lounge: The lounge with the fireplace right next to the Founder's Table.
Hilltop: The neighborhood just west of campus
Merlin: The huge, grizzled tree in Chapel Meadow
Mound Street: The fraternity house neighborhood
TA: Technology Assistant (help you with computer problems in

the dorms)
The Vooka: VUCA (Center for the Arts)
Voopdee: VUPD (Valparaiso University Police Department)
VUCRU: The student fan section at basketball games and other sporting events

Things I Wish I Knew Before Coming To School

- Go to FOCUS (freshman orientation).
- Hit up the Activities Fair each year for free stuff and good info.
- How strict RAs can be in the dorms.
- How unsatisfying the campus food can be.
- It's not a party school.
- None of the freshman dorms have air-conditioning.
- Specifics about Christ College.
- The classes are very challenging.

Tips to Succeed

- Check your e-mail, and then check it again.
- Get enough sleep or you're likely to get sick.
- Get used to community bathrooms.
- Go to class. Get used to studying more than you did in high school.
- Join Greek Life. Just get involved in all the organizations that Valpo has to offer.
- Learn the number for Domino's by heart.
- Learn to like college basketball.
- Take advantage of on-campus jobs.
- Talk to your profs—they are more than willing to help you.

Traditions

FOCUS: Each year, incoming freshmen attend this two-day orientation event held the summer before freshman year starts. This is a great way for students to meet other members of their class, find roommates, take placement exams, and meet with professors to talk about majors. Many freshmen end up remaining friends with fellow Foci for all four years at Valpo.

Late-Night Bingo: About once a month, the Union holds Late-Night Bingo from 11 p.m.–2 a.m. The proceeds go to charity, and students play for big prizes like TVs, DVD players, bicycles, gift certificates, and tons more. There are smaller prizes, too, such as baskets of candy and McDonald's certificates. This event has become so popular over the years that it had to change locations in order to accommodate the many people who wanted to play.

Midnight Madness: That's right, it's basketball again! Midnight Madness is held the midnight of the day when basketball practices can officially start as per NCAA rules. Thousands of fans and students gather at the ARC to watch the first practice of the men's and women's teams, including a scrimmage, slam dunk contest, and three-point contest. Tons of free prizes are given out and students are usually treated to a laser-light show and a meet-and-greet with the players.

Paint the Campus: During Homecoming, student groups and Greek organizations turn out to paint the windows of the Union and the dorms with their artistic renderings of the Homecoming theme. These are judged in a competition, and the winning team receives points toward their Homecoming total.

Sibling Weekend: Each winter, Valpo students host any and all of their siblings for a weekend of campus fun. The University shows kid-friendly movies and schedules multiple events that students can easily attend with siblings.

Songfest: Songfest is the culmination of Spring Week and is a contest between Greek organizations. It is basically a song-and-dance revue; each team choreographs a routine and chooses costumes. The performance is held in the Chapel, and it always promises to be a good time.

Vespers: These are special music-filled worship services held late at night during the Advent and Christmas seasons. Tickets disappear so quickly that some students go all four years without ever being able to attend. Even though they are held in the Chapel, which seats about 5,000 people, tickets are offered to the community and alumni as well, and they always sell out.

Urban Legends

- If you step on the seal in Berg Hall, you'll fail your finals. Go kiss the grave instead!

- In the 1920s, the Ku Klux Klan considered buying the University.
- Kiss the dog's grave on Old Campus for luck on finals.
- Kissing Bridge has moved a few times. The original legend was that if you kissed your sweetie on the bridge as a train passed below, you were soul mates.
- Legend has it that the administration nudged a group of students to create and implement the Honor Code system.

Students Speak Out On...
The Inside Scoop

Q Highly Academic and Fun
I know it is a university, but I was impressed by the academic strength here.

Q Small School, Big Opportunities
With its many study abroad opportunities, academic programs, and available funding from various institutions and departments, Valpo is a great place for anyone who wants a small campus atmosphere with big opportunities.

Q Profs. and Students
I enjoy the relationships one creates with their professors. Professors are so personable and really just want to see each student succeed and are willing to help the students in anyway possible. Also whole classes are invited to professors houses for dinner or breakfast around final exam time. How cool is that?!

Q The Hidden Wonder
Academics here are amazing. The professors really want to get to know you and help you out as much as possible. Plus, there is a lot going on on campus through union board and organizations-concerts, comedians, campus movies and other events. Greek life also offers a great way to be involved and really enjoy a good college experience while still learning and growing as an individual.

Q Friendly People
The people at Valpo are the friendliest people EVER!

Christ College
Christ College is the honors college and a wonderful addition to the college curriculum! The classes available are very interesting and diverse and add a lot to the liberal arts education.

Yay Valpo!
I love Valpo especially for the ease it offers as far as getting involved on campus. If you want to be a part of a club or organization there is usually no problem. I also love the study abroad opportunities and all the help the international office offers. I like the smaller student body because I feel like I see people I know all the time, but there is still plenty to do around campus.

Faith-Based Learning
I love that Valpo incorporates faith into everyday learning, but not in a forceful way. It means that we're applying our classes to real life, and the person we're becoming, not just doing what it takes to get the grade. Our professors genuinely care about us, and that helps us succeed as well.

Jobs & Internships

The Lowdown On...
Jobs & Internships

Career Center
1509 Chapel Dr.
(219) 464-5005
career.center@valpo.edu
www.valpo.edu/career

Employment Services?
Yes

Placement Services?
Yes

Other Career Services
Career counseling
Career fairs
Career resource library
Cooperative education
Experience eRecruiting
(online job search)
Job opportunities bulletin
Mock interviews
On-campus employer interviews
Résumé advising

Advice

The Career Center staff does its best to be helpful in your career search. However, it often seems like their programs and fairs reach out particularly to nursing, engineering, and business majors, with little help for anyone else. They have also included fairs for Law Schools and Graduate Schools, though, to apply to more students. If you need help creating or proofing your résumé or want to browse lists of internship opportunities, you'll want to become friends with a career counselor. Take advantage of the Career Center's reading room. They have books upon books and catalogs full of career advice and opportunities. Also, make sure you do go to the career fairs and do the networking thing, even if you're not particularly interested in any of the jobs offered—it's still a great way to make contacts.

Firms That Most Frequently Hire Grads

Caterpillar
Commonwealth Edison
Indiana Department of Transportation
KPMG LLP
Northwestern Memorial Hospital

Did You Know?

Best On-Campus Jobs for Students:

- Admissions Office
- Coffee shop
- Library
- Resident Assistant
- Student Research Assistant
- Teaching Assistant
- Writing Center Consultant

Worst On-Campus Jobs for Students:

- Banquet Setup/Cleanup
- Cashier
- Desk attendant
- Dining Services
- IT, especially the first week of school

Best Off-Campus Jobs for Students:

- Buffalo Wild Wings
- Domino's
- Jimmy Johns
- Retail
- Subway
- Target
- Wal-Mart

Alumni & Post-Grads

The Lowdown On...
Alumni & Post-Grads

Alumni Office
Office of Alumni Relations
Loke Hall
Phone: (800) 833-6792 x23
alumni@valpo.edu
www.valpo.edu/alumni

Major Alumni Events
Alumni Reunions
Homecoming

Services Available
The Valpo Alumni Association works with students through VAULT, the Valparaiso Undergraduate Alumni Leadership Organization. The alumni office provides an alumni e-mail directory and event calendar.

Alumni Publications
VALPO Magazine

Did You Know?

Famous VU Alumni:

- Bryce Drew (Class of '98) – NBA basketball player for the Houston Rockets, Charlotte Hornets, and Chicago Bulls
- Jackie Lyden (Class of '75) – Senior correspondent for NPR
- Lloyd McClendon (Class of '81) – Former manager of the Pittsburgh Pirates
- Al Seib (Class of '78) – Photojournalist, Los Angeles Times
- Kathi Seifert (Class of '71) – Executive Vice President, Kimberly-Clark Corporation

Student Organizations

The Lowdown On...

Clubs and Organizations on Campus
A complete list of Valparaiso's Student Organizations can be found on the University's Web site. There are about 100 different clubs to get involved in, and if you don't find what you are looking for, you can create a new one.

Student Organizations Web Site
www.valpo.edu/about_valpo/student_organizations.html

ROTC
Air Force ROTC: Yes
Navy ROTC: No
Army ROTC: Yes

Student Newspaper
The Torch

Student Activities Offered
Campus ministries
Choral groups
Concert band
Dance
Drama/theater
International student organizations
Jazz band
Literary magazine
Music ensembles
Musical theater
Pep band
Radio station
Student government
Student newspaper
Symphony orchestra
Yearbook

The Best

The **BEST** Things

1. Basketball

2. Free movies from Union Board

3. On-campus concerts

4. The library

5. Awesome academic programs

6. Great local restaurants

7. Quality profs

8. Cheap parking passes

9. Maria Elena's

10. Close to Chicago

The Worst

The **WORST** Things

1. Snow over two feet deep in the winter
2. Community bathrooms
3. VUPD
4. Rain and clouds—a lot of the time
5. Dining hall food
6. Finding a legal parking spot
7. Greeks taking over student government
8. Alcohol policy

The Lowdown On...
Visiting

Campus Tours
Contact the Office of Admissions to set up your personalized tour or visit, or take advantage of any of the visit days on campus.

Campus Map
www.valpo.edu/maps

Virtual Tour of Campus
www.valpo.edu/maps

Interviews & Information Sessions

Register for a Brown and Gold visit day via the Admissions Web site, or call (888) GO-VALPO Monday–Friday 8 a.m.–5 p.m.

Overnight Visits

Valpo Overnight Visits (VOV) can be scheduled by contacting Admissions. You'll get to stay in the dorms with a VOV host—a Valpo student. You can attend classes, meet with profs, and get a real taste of VU life.

Words to Know

Academic Probation – A suspension imposed on a student if he or she fails to keep up with the school's minimum academic requirements. Those unable to improve their grades after receiving this warning can face dismissal.

Beer Pong/Beirut – A drinking game involving cups of beer arranged in a pyramid shape on each side of a table. The goal is to get a ping pong ball into one of the opponent's cups by throwing the ball or hitting it with a paddle. If the ball lands in a cup, the opponent is required to drink the beer.

Bid – An invitation from a fraternity or sorority to 'pledge' (join) that specific house.

Blue-Light Phone – Brightly-colored phone posts with a blue light bulb on top. These phones exist for security purposes and are located at various outside locations around most campuses. In an emergency, a student can pick up one of these phones (free of charge) to connect with campus police or a security escort.

Campus Police – Police who are specifically assigned to a given institution. Campus police are typically not regular city officers; they are employed by the university in a full-time capacity.

Club Sports – A level of sports that falls somewhere between varsity and intramural. If a student is unable to commit to a varsity team but has a lot of passion for athletics, a club sport could be a better, less intense option. Even less demanding, intramural (IM) sports often involve no traveling and considerably less time.

Cocaine – An illegal drug. Also known as "coke" or "blow," cocaine often resembles a white crystalline or powdery substance. It is highly addictive and dangerous.

Common Application – An application with which students can apply to multiple schools.

Course Registration – The period of official class selection for the upcoming quarter or semester. Prior to registration, it is best to prepare several back-up courses in case a particular class becomes full. If a course is full, students can place themselves on the waitlist, although this still does not guarantee entry.

Division Athletics – Athletic classifications range from Division I to Division III. Division IA is the most competitive, while Division III is considered to be the least competitive.

Dorm – A dorm (or dormitory) is an on-campus housing facility. Dorms can provide a range of options from suite-style rooms to more communal options that include shared bathrooms. Most first-year students live in dorms. Some upperclassmen who wish to stay on campus also choose this option.

Early Action – An application option with which a student can apply to a school and receive an early acceptance response without a binding commitment. This system is becoming less and less available.

Early Decision – An application option that students should use only if they are certain they plan to attend the school in question. If a student applies using the early decision option and is admitted, he or she is required and bound to attend that university. Admission rates are usually higher among students who apply through early decision, as the student is clearly indicating that the school is his or her first choice.

Ecstasy – An illegal drug. Also known as "E" or "X," ecstasy looks like a pill and most resembles an aspirin. Considered a party drug, ecstasy is very dangerous and can be deadly.

Ethernet – An extremely fast Internet connection available in most university-owned residence halls. To use an Ethernet connection properly, a student will need a network card and cable for his or her computer.

Fake ID – A counterfeit identification card that contains false information. Most commonly, students get fake IDs with altered birthdates so that they appear to be older than 21 (and therefore of legal drinking age). Even though it is illegal, many college students have fake IDs in hopes of purchasing alcohol or getting into bars.

Frosh – Slang for "freshman" or "freshmen."

Hazing – Initiation rituals administered by some fraternities or sororities as part of the pledging process. Many universities have outlawed hazing due to its degrading, and sometimes dangerous, nature.

Intramurals (IMs) – A popular, and usually free, sport league in which students create teams and compete against one another. These sports vary in competitiveness and can include a range of activities—everything from billiards to water polo. IM sports are a great way to meet people with similar interests.

Keg – Officially called a half-barrel, a keg contains roughly 200 12-ounce servings of beer.

LSD – An illegal drug, also known as acid, this hallucinogenic drug most commonly resembles a tab of paper.

Marijuana – An illegal drug, also known as weed or pot; along with alcohol, marijuana is one of the most commonly found drugs on campuses across the country.

Major – The focal point of a student's college studies; a specific topic that is studied for a degree. Examples of majors include physics, English, history, computer science, economics, business, and music. Many students decide on a specific major before arriving on campus, while others are simply "undecided" until declaring a major. Those who are extremely interested in two areas can also choose to double major.

Meal Block – The equivalent of one meal. Students on a meal plan usually receive a fixed number of meals per week. Each meal, or "block," can be redeemed at the school's dining facilities in place of cash. Often, a student's weekly allotment of meal blocks will be forfeited if not used.

Minor – An additional focal point in a student's education. Often serving as a complement or addition to a student's main area of focus, a minor has fewer requirements and prerequisites to fulfill than a major. Minors are not required for graduation from most schools; however some students who want to explore many different interests choose to pursue both a major and a minor.

Mushrooms – An illegal drug. Also known as "'shrooms," this drug resembles regular mushrooms but is extremely hallucinogenic.

Off-Campus Housing – Housing from a particular landlord or rental group that is not affiliated with the university. Depending on the college, off-campus housing can range from extremely popular to non-existent. Students who choose to live off campus are typically given more freedom, but they also have to deal with possible subletting scenarios, furniture, bills, and other issues. In addition to these factors, rental prices and distance often affect a student's decision to move off campus.

Office Hours – Time that teachers set aside for students who have questions about coursework. Office hours are a good forum for students to go over any problems and to show interest in the subject material.

Pledging – The early phase of joining a fraternity or sorority, pledging takes place after a student has gone through rush and received a bid. Pledging usually lasts between one and two semesters. Once the pledging period is complete and a particular student has done everything that is required to become a member, that student is considered a brother or sister. If a fraternity or a sorority would decide to "haze" a group of students, this initiation would take place during the pledging period.

Private Institution – A school that does not use tax revenue to subsidize education costs. Private schools typically cost more than public schools and are usually smaller.

Prof – Slang for "professor."

Public Institution – A school that uses tax revenue to subsidize education costs. Public schools are often a good value for in-state residents and tend to be larger than most private colleges.

Quarter System (or Trimester System) – A type of academic calendar system. In this setup, students take classes for three academic periods. The first quarter usually starts in late September or early October and concludes right before Christmas. The second quarter usually starts around early to mid–January and finishes up around March or April. The last academic quarter, or "third quarter," usually starts in late March or early April and finishes up in late May or Mid-June. The fourth quarter is summer. The major difference between the quarter system and semester system is that students take more, less comprehensive courses under the quarter calendar.

RA (Resident Assistant) – A student leader who is assigned to a particular floor in a dormitory in order to help to the other students who live there. An RA's duties include ensuring student safety and providing assistance wherever possible.

Recitation – An extension of a specific course; a review session. Some classes, particularly large lectures, are supplemented with mandatory recitation sessions that provide a relatively personal class setting.

Rolling Admissions – A form of admissions. Most commonly found at public institutions, schools with this type of policy continue to accept students throughout the year until their class sizes are met. For example, some schools begin accepting students as early as December and will continue to do so until April or May.

Room and Board – This figure is typically the combined cost of a university-owned room and a meal plan.

Room Draw/Housing Lottery – A common way to pick on-campus room assignments for the following year. If a student decides to remain in university-owned housing, he or she is assigned a unique number that, along with seniority, is used to determine his or her housing for the next year.

Rush – The period in which students can meet the brothers and sisters of a particular chapter and find out if a given fraternity or sorority is right for them. Rushing a fraternity or a sorority is not a requirement at any school. The goal of rush is to give students who are serious about pledging a feel for what to expect.

Semester System – The most common type of academic calendar system at college campuses. This setup typically includes two semesters in a given school year. The fall semester starts around the end of August or early September and concludes before winter vacation. The spring semester usually starts in mid-January and ends in late April or May.

Student Center/Rec Center/Student Union – A common area on campus that often contains study areas, recreation facilities, and eateries. This building is often a good place to meet up with fellow students; depending on the school, the student center can have a huge role or a non-existent role in campus life.

Student ID – A university-issued photo ID that serves as a student's key to school-related functions. Some schools require students to show these cards in order to get into dorms, libraries, cafeterias, and other facilities. In addition to storing meal plan information, in some cases, a student ID can actually work as a debit card and allow students to purchase things from bookstores or local shops.

Suite – A type of dorm room. Unlike dorms that feature communal bathrooms shared by the entire floor, suites offer bathrooms shared only among the suite. Suite-style dorm rooms can house anywhere from two to ten students.

TA (Teacher's Assistant) – An undergraduate or grad student who helps in some manner with a specific course. In some cases, a TA will teach a class, assist a professor, grade assignments, or conduct office hours.

Undergraduate – A student in the process of studying for his or her bachelor's degree.

About the Author

Name: Amber Will

Hometown: Schofield, WI

Major: Political Science and History

Fun Fact: I am a die hard Packers fan... but I still love Brett Favre!

Previous Contributors: Matthew A. Stevens

Pros and Cons

Still can't figure out if this is the right school for you? You've already read through this in-depth guide; why not list the pros and cons? It will really help with narrowing down your decision and determining whether or not this school is right for you.

Pros	Cons
....	....
....	....
....	....
....	....
....	....
....	....
....	....
....	....
....	....
....	....
....	....
....	....

Pros and Cons

Still can't figure out if this is the right school for you? You've already read through this in-depth guide; why not list the pros and cons? It will really help with narrowing down your decision and determining whether or not this school is right for you.

Pros	**Cons**
....	....
....	....
....	....
....	....
....	....
....	....
....	....
....	....
....	....
....	....
....	....
....	....

Notes

Notes

Notes

Notes

Notes

Notes

Notes

Notes

Notes

Notes

Notes

Notes

Notes

Notes

College Scholarships

Search. Apply. Win!

 College Prowler gives away thousands of dollars each month through our popular monthly scholarships, including our $2,000 "No Essay" scholarship.

Plus, we'll connect you with hundreds of other scholarships based on your unique information and qualifications!

Create a College Prowler account today to get matched with millions of dollars in relevant scholarships!

**Sign up and apply now at
<u>www.collegeprowler.com/register</u>**

Review Your School!

Let your voice be heard.

Every year, thousands of students take our online survey to share their opinions about campus life.

Now's your chance to help millions of high school students choose the right college for them.

Tell us what life is really like at your school by taking our online survey or even uploading your own photos and videos!

And as our thanks to you for participating in our survey, we'll enter you into a random drawing for our $1,000 Monthly Survey Scholarship!

For more information, check out
www.collegeprowler.com/survey

Write For Us!

Express your opinion. Get published!

Interested in being a published author? College Prowler is always on the lookout for current college students across the country to write the guides for their schools.

The contributing author position is a unique opportunity for eager college students to bolster their résumés and portfolios, become published authors both online and in print, and gain tremendous exposure to millions of high school students nationwide.

For more details, visit
www.collegeprowler.com/careers

Order now! • *collegeprowler.com* • (800) 290-2682
More than 400 single-school guides available!

- Albion College
- Alfred University
- Allegheny College
- Alverno College
- American Intercontinental University Online
- American University
- Amherst College
- Arizona State University
- Ashford University
- The Art Institute of California – Orange County
- Auburn University
- Austin College
- Babson College
- Ball State University
- Bard College
- Barnard College
- Barry University
- Baruch College
- Bates College
- Bay Path College
- Baylor University
- Beloit College
- Bentley University
- Berea College
- Binghamton University
- Birmingham Southern College
- Bob Jones University
- Boston College
- Boston University
- Bowdoin College
- Bradley University
- Brandeis University
- Brigham Young University
- Brigham Young University – Idaho
- Brown University
- Bryant University
- Bryn Mawr College
- Bucknell University
- Cal Poly Pomona
- California College of the Arts
- California Institute of Technology
- California Polytechnic State University
- California State University – Monterey Bay
- California State University – Northridge
- California State University – San Marcos
- Carleton College
- Carnegie Mellon University
- Case Western Reserve University
- Catawba College
- Catholic University of America
- Centenary College of Louisiana
- Centre College
- Chapman University
- Chatham University
- City College of New York
- City College of San Francisco
- Claflin University
- Claremont McKenna College
- Clark Atlanta University
- Clark University
- Clemson University
- Cleveland State University
- Colby College
- Colgate University
- College of Charleston
- College of Mount Saint Vincent
- College of Notre Dame of Maryland
- College of the Holy Cross
- College of William & Mary
- College of Wooster
- Colorado College
- Columbia College Chicago
- Columbia University
- Concordia University – Wisconsin
- Connecticut College
- Contra Costa College
- Cornell College
- Cornell University
- Creighton University
- CUNY Lehman College
- CUNY Queens College
- CUNY Queensborough Community College
- Dalton State College
- Dartmouth College
- Davidson College
- De Anza College
- Del Mar College
- Denison University
- DePaul University
- DePauw University
- Diablo Valley College
- Dickinson College
- Dordt College
- Drexel University
- Duke University
- Duquesne University
- Earlham College
- East Carolina University
- Eckerd College
- El Paso Community College
- Elon University
- Emerson College
- Emory University
- Fashion Institute of Design & Merchandising
- Fashion Institute of Technology
- Ferris State University
- Florida Atlantic University
- Florida Southern College
- Florida State University
- Fordham University
- Franklin & Marshall College
- Franklin Pierce University
- Frederick Community College
- Freed-Hardeman University
- Furman University
- Gannon University
- Geneva College
- George Mason University
- George Washington University
- Georgetown University
- Georgia Institute of Technology
- Georgia Perimeter College
- Georgia State University
- Germanna Community College
- Gettysburg College
- Gonzaga University
- Goucher College
- Grinnell College
- Grove City College
- Guilford College
- Gustavus Adolphus College
- Hamilton College
- Hampshire College
- Hampton University
- Hanover College
- Harvard University
- Harvey Mudd College
- Hastings College
- Haverford College
- Hillsborough Community College
- Hofstra University
- Hollins University
- Howard University
- Hunter College (CUNY)
- Idaho State University
- Illinois State University
- Illinois Wesleyan University
- Indiana Univ.–Purdue Univ. Indianapolis (IUPUI)
- Indiana University
- Iowa State University
- Ithaca College
- Jackson State University
- James Madison University
- Johns Hopkins University
- Juniata College
- Kansas State University
- Kaplan University
- Kent State University
- Kenyon College
- La Roche College
- Lafayette College
- Lawrence University
- Lehigh University
- Lewis & Clark College
- Linfield College
- Los Angeles City College
- Los Angeles Valley College
- Louisiana College
- Louisiana State University
- Loyola College in Maryland
- Loyola Marymount University
- Loyola University Chicago
- Luther College
- Macalester College
- Macomb Community College
- Manhattan College
- Manhattanville College
- Marlboro College
- Marquette University
- Maryville University
- Massachusetts College of Art & Design
- Massachusetts Institute of Technology
- McGill University
- Merced College
- Mercyhurst College
- Messiah College
- Miami University
- Michigan State University
- Middle Tennessee State University
- Middlebury College
- Millsaps College
- Minnesota State University – Moorhead
- Missouri State University
- Montana State University
- Montclair State University
- Moorpark College
- Mount Holyoke College
- Muhlenberg College
- New College of Florida
- New York University
- North Carolina A&T State University
- North Carolina State University
- Northeastern University
- Northern Arizona University
- Northern Illinois University
- Northwest Florida State College
- Northwestern College – Saint Paul
- Northwestern University

Oakwood University
Oberlin College
Occidental College
Oglethorpe University
Ohio State University
Ohio University
Ohio Wesleyan University
Old Dominion University
Onondaga Community College
Oral Roberts University
Pace University
Palm Beach State College
Penn State Altoona
Penn State Brandywine
Penn State University
Pepperdine University
Pitzer College
Pomona College
Princeton University
Providence College
Purdue University
Radford University
Ramapo College of New Jersey
Reed College
Rensselaer Polytechnic Institute
Rhode Island School of Design
Rhodes College
Rice University
Rider University
Robert Morris University
Rochester Institute of Technology
Rocky Mountain College of Art & Design
Rollins College
Rowan University
Rutgers University
Sacramento State
Saint Francis University
Saint Joseph's University
Saint Leo University
Salem College
Salisbury University
Sam Houston State University
Samford University
San Diego State University
San Francisco State University
Santa Clara University
Santa Fe College
Sarah Lawrence College
Scripps College
Seattle University
Seton Hall University
Simmons College
Skidmore College
Slippery Rock University
Smith College

South Texas College
Southern Methodist University
Southwestern University
Spelman College
St. John's College – Annapolis
St. John's University
St. Louis University
St. Mary's University
St. Olaf College
Stanford University
State University of New York – Purchase College
State University of New York at Fredonia
State University of New York at Oswego
Stetson University
Stevens-Henager College
Stony Brook University (SUNY)
Susquehanna University
Swarthmore College
Syracuse University
Taylor University
Temple University
Tennessee State University
Texas A&M University
Texas Christian University
Texas Tech
The Community College of Baltimore County
Towson University
Trinity College (Conn.)
Trinity University (Texas)
Troy University
Truman State University
Tufts University
Tulane University
Union College
University at Albany (SUNY)
University at Buffalo (SUNY)
University of Alabama
University of Arizona
University of Arkansas
University of Arkansas at Little Rock
University of California – Berkeley
University of California – Davis
University of California – Irvine
University of California – Los Angeles
University of California – Merced
University of California – Riverside
University of California – San Diego

University of California – Santa Barbara
University of California – Santa Cruz
University of Central Florida
University of Chicago
University of Cincinnati
University of Colorado
University of Connecticut
University of Delaware
University of Denver
University of Florida
University of Georgia
University of Hartford
University of Illinois
University of Illinois at Chicago
University of Iowa
University of Kansas
University of Kentucky
University of Louisville
University of Maine
University of Maryland
University of Maryland – Baltimore County
University of Massachusetts
University of Miami
University of Michigan
University of Minnesota
University of Mississippi
University of Missouri
University of Montana
University of Mount Union
University of Nebraska
University of Nevada – Las Vegas
University of New Hampshire
University of North Carolina
University of North Carolina – Greensboro
University of Notre Dame
University of Oklahoma
University of Oregon
University of Pennsylvania
University of Phoenix
University of Pittsburgh
University of Puget Sound
University of Rhode Island
University of Richmond
University of Rochester
University of San Diego
University of San Francisco
University of South Carolina
University of South Dakota
University of South Florida
University of Southern California
University of St Thomas – Texas

University of Tampa
University of Tennessee
University of Tennessee at Chattanooga
University of Texas
University of Utah
University of Vermont
University of Virginia
University of Washington
University of Western Ontario
University of Wisconsin
University of Wisconsin – Stout
Urbana University
Ursinus College
Valencia Community College
Valparaiso University
Vanderbilt University
Vassar College
Villanova University
Virginia Commonwealth University
Virginia Tech
Virginia Union University
Wagner College
Wake Forest University
Warren Wilson College
Washington & Jefferson College
Washington & Lee University
Washington University in St. Louis
Wellesley College
Wesleyan University
West Los Angeles College
West Point Military Academy
West Virginia University
Western Illinois University
Western Kentucky University
Wheaton College (Ill.)
Wheaton College (Mass.)
Whitman College
Wilkes University
Willamette University
Williams College
Xavier University
Yale University
Youngstown State University

Order now! • collegeprowler.com • (800) 290-2682
More than 400 single-school guides available!

CPSIA information can be obtained at www.ICGtesting.com
Printed in the USA
LVOW122023010412

275410LV00001B/19/P